How to Make Money
Publishing from Home

How to Make Money Publishing from Home

Everything You Need to Know to Successfully Publish Books, Newsletters, Web Sites, Greeting Cards, and Software

Revised Second Edition

Lisa Shaw

PRIMA PUBLISHING

3000 Lava Ridge Court • Roseville, California 95661
(800) 632-8676 • www.primalifestyles.com

PRIMA PUBLISHING and colophon are trademarks of Prima Communications Inc., registered with the United States Patent and Trademark Office.

Disclaimer

This book contains information of a general nature regarding starting and operating a business. It is not intended as a substitute for professional, legal, or financial advice. As laws may vary from state to state, readers should consult a competent legal or financial professional regarding their own particular business. In addition, readers should understand that the business world is highly dynamic and contains certain risks. Therefore, the author and publisher cannot warrant or guarantee that the use of any information contained in this book will work in any given situation.

Library of Congress Cataloging-in-Publication Data
Shaw, Lisa Angowski Rogak.
How to make money publishing from home : everything you need to know to successfully publish books, newsletters, Web sites, greeting cards, and software / Lisa Shaw.—2nd ed.
    p. cm.
Includes index.
ISBN 0-7615-2169-0
1. Publishers and publishing—United States—Management. 2. Home-based businesses—United States—Management. 3. Desktop publishing industry—United States—Management. I. Title
Z471.S445 2000
070.5'068—dc21   99–057315
                                                                CIP

00 01 02 03 BB 10 9 8 7 6 5 4 3 2 1

Printed in the United States of America

HOW TO ORDER
Single copies may be ordered from Prima Publishing, 3000 Lava Ridge Court, Roseville, CA 95661; telephone (800) 632-8676. Quantity discounts are also available. On your letterhead, include information concerning the intended use of the books and the number of books you wish to purchase.

Visit us online at www.primalifestyles.com

For Lyle Lovett and His Large Band,
for helping to make the late nights
seem not so bad . . .

Contents

✦

Introduction

✦

FOR THE most part, I've always worked for myself, running my own publishing business out of my home since 1981. It hasn't always been easy, especially in the days before the first crude desktop publishing software programs became available, but I've always preferred to work for myself than to work for someone else. Whether publishing newsletters, writing books, producing computer software, or creating and selling a line of greeting cards, I've done well, in part because I've been able to call the shots as to what I produce, where I work, and how I work. For me, that means that I can live in a rural area, work at home surrounded by my six cats, and let voice mail pick up whenever I'm feeling particularly antisocial.

In the past, whenever I've accepted a regular job—that is, working in an office for somebody else—my tenure was inevitably short. I either got fired or quit after a month or two. Rather than a regular paycheck, I have preferred to rely on my own efforts and be poor but free. I've managed to stick it out long enough that I am making some money and I'm still free—to a certain extent.

In the two decades that I've been running my own home-based publishing business, I've run into a lot of people who don't understand why I do what I do. And once *you* start your own business, there's a good chance that you'll run into the same kind of people, those who would rather give up their freedom and creativity in order to possess that elusive thing known as "security" as well as some degree of status within that field. More often than not, they resent people like you and me, those who are willing to take the chance to be happy with their work.

Yes, money—or the lack of it—also enters into the equation, but you'll quickly discover that you need more than money to get a home-based publishing business off the ground and keep it growing. Having adequate money to start and run your business can actually be a handicap because it's easy to rely on dollars first and effort second.

In fact, I had no money in my early publishing ventures, so I had to rely solely on my creativity and my intractable faith in my own abilities. In other words, I'm stubborn and independent to a fault: If I wanted to make something happen, I couldn't wait around for someone else to do it because *it wasn't gonna happen.*

Regardless of the type of publishing business you're thinking about starting, this book will provide you with lots of information on financing, business planning, marketing, and legal and tax issues, along with the day-to-day considerations of running a business. And, of course, I include lots of ideas about specific types of home-based publishing businesses.

So start dreaming about the type of home-based publishing business you'd like to run.

How to Make Money
Publishing from Home

PART ONE

The Home-Based Publishing Industry

Why Run a Home Publishing Business Now?

✦

THESE DAYS, it seems that trends come from out of nowhere and garner a lot of press overnight. All eyes turn toward whatever happens to be hot at the moment, from new concepts in the business world to the latest Internet IPO. Such fads are usually very popular for awhile and then either fade into the background as people become blasé about them or disappear entirely as their primary appeal wears off.

On the surface, that's how it would appear to be with a home-based publishing business. "Yeah," you may think, "it's great to work at home, publish anything you want, and make some money besides, but just

wait and see, it'll never catch on." Such perceptions are understandable but inaccurate. Though running your own home-based publishing business is a radical departure from working in the traditional corporate structure as Americans have slavishly done for the last 100 years—a practice we have only recently begun to abandon in significant numbers—all the signs suggest that this new form of independent publishing is catching on permanently.

The advent and quick development of technology and the seemingly magical things you can do with computers—that today are a tiny fraction of the size and price of the computers of twenty years ago—have largely been responsible for the growing popularity of home-based publishing businesses. As surely as computers will continue to be obsolete the minute you walk out of the store, the power of today's and tomorrow's computers will continue to allow people to work more effectively, and quickly, and to live and run their publishing businesses anywhere they want, even out of a tepee.

The Internet and the World Wide Web, along with e-mail, fax machines, and overnight delivery services, have brought the world to us no matter where we live. Instead of having to leave home and slog through stacks of books, journals, and periodicals to locate the information we desire, we can now conduct research and market our businesses from home, 24 hours a day. It's been three years since I renewed my library card at Dartmouth College, a 35-mile trek from my house. No need to, since I can find everything I need to know by logging onto the Internet.

Of course, some people still regard working and running a business from home as a radical concept. But the U.S. economy has long been in the process of converting itself from a manufacturing base to one that values information. This means that entrepreneurs who are able to provide people with the information they're looking for—in the form of a book, newsletter, on computer disk, or in another form—will have no trouble thriving with lots of hard work, creative mar-

keting, superb customer service, and a little bit of luck and timing.

Home-Based Publishing: A Growing Trend

RUNNING A home-based publishing business is catching on across the country for a number of reasons.

Futurist Alvin Toffler, author of *Future Shock* and *The Third Wave*, spent years telling Americans that millions of us would soon be working at home in what he dubbed "electronic cottages." He also foresaw that information would become the currency that drives the American economy and predicted that massive urban office buildings would stand empty amidst formerly bustling downtowns, but this hasn't come to pass—yet.

Long commutes to an outside office consume time, money, and energy, and make people less productive not only at work but at home. Additional time is usually required each day and on the weekend to decompress from the stresses of the week. Running your own publishing business from your home eliminates some if not all of this stress. And, of course, being your own boss has become the dream of millions of Americans. Here are some other benefits:

✦ Rural residents are starting their own home-based publishing businesses in increasing numbers because they want to make more money than they could otherwise earn in their relatively isolated areas. By working for themselves and focusing on a national market, instead of a local one, people who run home-based publishing businesses and live in the country not only can earn a decent living but may also stimulate the economy in regions that are traditionally depressed.

◆ More people want to pursue interests that they're really passionate about, including hobbies, part-time and/or seasonal businesses, even education. In other words, they want to do more than just spend most of their waking hours at work. Running a home-based publishing business can save hours each day by eliminating travel time. The time saved can be spent on these outside pursuits, and with friends and family.

◆ Finally, people who run home-based publishing businesses can save a significant amount of money because they're not paying for lunches out, tolls, gas, parking, and appropriate clothes to wear to the office.

The Influence of the Internet

THERE ARE numerous reasons why a growing number of people are publishing their own works—and those of others—from home, but perhaps the most pervasive reason is the Internet, and its ability to easily and inexpensively reach people all over the world and from all walks of life. No longer is it necessary for aspiring publishers to postpone producing a book, newsletter, or article for financial or logistical reasons. Now you can write your book, post it online—or make it available in one of the many online venues where buyers can purchase your book by downloading it—concentrate on getting the word out instead of worrying about inventory.

Powerful software also makes it easy to incorporate detailed graphics and design an attractive Web page or e-newsletter that can fully capture people's attention and encourage them to read more of your work in the future.

More people online means that Internet venues are starved for content: yours. Internet publishing entrepreneurs everywhere are striking deals with Web site managers, supplying the sites with new content in exchange for a plug, creating a vibrant marketplace that's open to anyone with a modem.

Technology changes so quickly, however, that what is new this month becomes ordinary the next. If you, as a home-based publisher, can manage to keep on top of the technology, you'll be well on the way to growing your business.

Why Are More People Interested in Running a Home-Based Publishing Business?

WHEN ASKED whether they would like to start their own home-based publishing business, people who love to read and who love the idea of actually creating the written word usually respond with an enthusiastic, "Sure!" Their minds then start to race with thoughts of being their own boss, producing their own literature, and having an audience of avid readers who are eager for their opinions and ideas. Unfortunately, what frequently happens is that after the initial rush of dreaming about running their own businesses, they immediately start thinking of all of the reasons why they *won't* be able to pull it off.

But the fact is that more people are overcoming their doubts and are actively making plans to start their own home-based publishing businesses and here's why:

✦ *The desire to accomplish what* you *want to do for a change.* Several generations of Americans have been unfairly branded as selfish. The truth is that many people—especially women—are more selfless than the media makes them out to be. Here, too, people seek balance: In order to give to others, you have to give to yourself as well. Following your dreams by working from home and running your own publishing business is a great way to start.

✦ *The desire to break through the glass ceiling or rise above the sticky floor.* If you haven't already "made it" in your current field or job, your chances of ever reaching the upper echelons of your company or industry probably aren't that great—unless you start doing things in a radically different manner. This is often the point when people start to investigate the possibility of starting their own business, and a publishing venture at that, if they've long wanted to impart information to the world.

✦ *The desire to explore a particular interest in depth.* When you're young and idealistic, it's easy to think you'll be able to reach your career goals by the time you hit the age of 25. In most cases, of course, real life intercedes, and the need to make a living pushes your main focus to the back burner, where it remains until retirement, if it manages to resurface at all. But sometimes, everyday life—the job, the family, the bills—just becomes too much to bear, and you figure, "Dammit, I work hard, why shouldn't I be able to do what I want?" By working from home and running your own publishing business, you'll be able to explore your own interests and make money at it besides.

◆ *Refusal to buy into the corporate structure.* Millions of baby boomers poured into the mainstream labor markets in the 1970s and 1980s. Some immediately saw all the warts and left; most decided to stick it out. But when things didn't get much better, they decided to take matters into their own hands by starting their own businesses from their home offices, where they could get their work done in peace and quiet, and avoid the constant onslaught of office politics that seems to consume so much of the typical employee's day.

No doubt at least one of your reasons for wanting to start your own home-based publishing business is listed above. Some of you might agree with every item on the list, yet remain convinced that the best thing to do is to suffer in silence—you need your job and you don't want to jeopardize it, you have too many bills, and . . . .

Stop! Don't think like this. Once you declare your intention to start your own home-based publishing business, you're well on your way. However, don't be surprised if you receive some negative reactions from family and friends, who may also want to start their own businesses but haven't done it yet. There's a good chance that if they see you start to pursue your own dreams they'll view you as disturbing the status quo. "What makes you think

you're better than the rest of us?" they may ask—that is, if they even have the guts to bring it up with you. "Why do you think you have what it takes to do what you want if the rest of us can't?"

The fact is you're not just like the rest; by picking up a copy of this book, you're taking a step toward living the life that you really want to live.

The Benefits of Running a Home-Based Publishing Business

HERE ARE just some of the advantages that you will enjoy by starting your own home-based publishing business:

◆ Less commuting time, more time to work and play.

◆ More time for yourself and your family.

◆ More time for leisure pursuits.

◆ Less stress, better health.

◆ Less money spent on gas, clothes, and meals out.

The Disadvantages of Running a Home-Based Publishing Business

OF COURSE, even though working from home is wonderful in many ways, there are a few disadvantages, and it's not for everyone. Even the most content home-based publishers admit to some downsides of running their businesses from home:

+ You may feel isolated if you work by yourself.

+ You may find it difficult to motivate yourself.

+ You may find that it's hard to stop working at the end of the day.

+ Your neighbors may drop in to socialize, and you may find it hard to turn them away.

+ It may be hard to resist the refrigerator, TV, or other distractions in your home.

+ It may take awhile until the business starts to generate revenue.

With a little effort, as well as an awareness of the disadvantages, you'll be well-armed to deal with them when they do arise.

Taking Stock Of Your Home-Based Publishing Business

◆

IF YOU want to start your own home-based publishing business, the first thing you should know is that you probably already possess all the skills that you'll need to be a success. You just need to do a bit of homework first.

The first thing to do is to figure out why you want to run your own publishing business. Next, try to be realistic about your expectations while acknowledging that it will be difficult at times.

Income and Profit Potentials

AS IS THE case with any new business, when you first start out, it may seem as though you're working for free, as you pour every penny of revenue back into your home-based publishing business—paying for a new computer system and more advanced software, or for brochures, or for copy paper.

Don't worry. Most new home-based publishing entrepreneurs find themselves in this dilemma at one time or another. It's unlikely that you'll have to invest huge amounts of cash upfront, or that you'll tie up a significant amount of money from the beginning in overhead or inventory like other businesses; if you work hard at keeping your expenses down while increasing your revenue with inexpensive marketing techniques, in time you'll be able to farm more work out and pay yourself a salary as well.

The amount of money you'll be able to realize from your business depends on a number of factors: how much marketing you'll do and how effective it will be, the universal audience for your products and publications, and the directions in which you'll later choose to branch out, whether by offering more specialized services to your customers or by expanding your customer base, depending on the type of home-based publishing business you plan to run.

Of course, hiring an employee or subcontracting some of the work to other businesses will increase your expenses. At the same time, it will free up some of your time so that you can concentrate on tasks that will bring in more business and more revenue, if indeed, that is what you would like to focus on. If you can, leave the grunt work—the chores and tasks that you don't like to do—to someone else, such as a mailing house for sorting and stuffing your bulk mailings.

Risk Potential

ANYONE WHO starts a publishing business from their home will face a certain amount of risk. Though statistics say that 90 percent of new businesses won't make it through their fifth anniversaries, the survival rate for home-based

publishing businesses that start with little or no capital, ironically, is much healthier.

You see, one problem that frequently occurs when people have money to invest in a small business is that they want to feel like they're running a business—with all the overhead it implies—and not be relegated to running their operations from a corner of the kitchen table. Even though they may not have any clients or business lined up on day one, I've heard of many instances where a publishing entrepreneur has spent thousands of dollars on fancy office furniture, rent, and complicated phone systems for their home offices. Two years later, they're nowhere to be seen. Why? Because they thought it was more important to assume the trappings of entrepreneurs who have been in business for awhile and therefore have *earned* the money to furnish their offices, instead of plowing all their money back into the business so that they could generate more business and more revenue.

Your chances of making it to your fifth anniversary are much improved if the focus of your business is suitably narrow, you've determined that your audience is large enough for the topic and information you plan to offer, and you provide a product or publication that reaches an audience that is not being adequately served.

Look in the obvious places to find your competition: in your town and region, in industry publications, and at associations.

Look at how they run their businesses to see what works and what doesn't. What are they not doing that you think they should? What techniques do they employ that you feel would work in your own business? Use this information to define the theme of your own business, publications, and products to increase your chances of success in the field. The good news is that if you find several competitors who cover the same ground that you plan to, the audience is probably large enough to support one more business—*yours*.

Assessing Your Personal Goals

BEFORE YOU start running your own home-based publishing business, take some time to evaluate yourself, your financial situation, and the skills you'll need to succeed. Doing your homework at this stage will save you from making big and possibly costly mistakes down the road.

First, determine what your overall personal goals are and how running your own home-based publishing business fits in with them—and vice versa.

Take some time to answer the following questions in detail:

+ What are the three main reasons why you want to run your own home-based publishing business?

+ How long to you plan to run y business?

+ Do you view your business as a part- or a full-time endeavor?

+ What are your personal goals, aside from running your business? Do you plan to retire at a certain age or move on to something else after running the business for five or ten years?

As you've already discovered, the fantasy of running your own business does not even begin to match the reality of the hard work that's required, even though you probably won't fully admit to this until you're knee-deep in the business. Many home-based publishing entrepreneurs succeed by viewing their businesses as a means to an end: It will provide them with a livelihood where they can have some control over their lives, or it may present the only way that they can finally live where they want to and be able to make a decent living. Or you may be working for a paltry salary while your boss sits back and just deposits the checks in the bank. If you were in charge of running your own home-based publishing business, you'd still be busting your butt, but at least you'd be getting paid fairly for it and you'd be able to make all of the decisions.

Other people dream of the self-sufficiency they'll be able to achieve by running their own business. Certainly some people who want to give up long

atisfying job or who
time with their fami-
k about becoming a
ng entrepreneur for

Running your own home-based publishing business is like any other job: You
need it to provide income along with a
healthy dose of satisfaction. But you also
need to have something in your life
besides the business. That's why it's
important to set goals for yourself that are
totally separate from the business.
Burnout is very common when you run
your own business, whether or not you
run it from your home or you're in the
publishing field, and one way to prevent
burnout is to set your personal goals—
that is, those that have absolutely nothing
to do with your business—in advance,
whether you want to learn a foreign language, or spend more time with your
friends and family. If you run your own
home-based publishing business, taking a
break is both possible and very necessary.

Assessing Your Financial Goals

I F Y O U want to get rich, you can buy
a book that says it will give you all the
secrets—but you'll still have to buy an
occasional lottery ticket. If you want to
have a decent income while you build
equity and increase your revenues a little

bit each year, keep reading. You're on the
right track in wanting to start your own
home-based publishing business.

To see whether your financial goals
jive with the goal of running your own
publishing business from your home, ask
yourself the following questions:

✦ What would you rather have after ten
years of hard work: a large sum of
money in the bank or equity in a valuable business that would be relatively
easy to sell?

✦ What's the least amount of money you
could live on each month, including
mortgage, taxes, and utilities?

✦ Do you like doing just one thing to
make a living, or do you prefer to juggle a variety of tasks?

For most people who decide to run
their own home-based publishing business, initially, money is usually a secondary concern. Of course, it takes money to
get a business up and running, but most
people who dream of starting their own
business are looking for the lifestyle and
satisfaction first and the income second.
These priorities will help keep you motivated when the money is slow and your
client list is taking longer to grow than
you had expected.

After the uncertainties of your first
year in business, you may feel you can
relax a little—the revenue may be a bit
more steady and you know what to expect

from your expenses—but you'll probably still find that it's necessary to reinvest much of your income back into the business in order to keep it growing. Because of this, unless you have a trust fund or a sizable side income, or hold onto your job or live off a spouse or partner's income, you must learn to live frugally and get used to the idea of being cash-poor, at least for awhile.

Many people who would like to start their own home-based publishing businesses shy away from it for financial reasons; they can't see risking part of their hard-earned savings or paycheck on a business that may or may not make any money for them. Even though you may be primarily motivated by the thought of being your own boss, running a business is all about financial risk—again, at least in the beginning. However, the possible payoff is great; financial success and personal satisfaction will come your way if you stick with an idea that is popular with a particular market. Therefore, if you want to have a good income in time, or even a great one, go ahead and start your own business. If you'd rather play it tried-and-true and feel safer with your money in a CD or savings account, then don't, because even though you may go into your business with a thick stack of contracts and assurances of work from people who are already familiar with your abilities, there will be days when things are going to be hairy. In the end, if you're per-sistent and think creatively, you'll be able to reach your financial goals as a home-based entrepreneur with no problem.

Assessing Your Tolerance for Risk

MANY PEOPLE who dream of running their own home-based publishing business love the idea and constantly fantasize about it, but when it comes right down to it, most will never take the necessary steps because they're reluctant to leave the security of a regular job, health insurance, the familiarity of a particular lifestyle—you name it—even if they're unhappy with their current lives. A person who falls into this category has a low tolerance for risk of any kind.

On the other hand, a person who can tolerate risk and who even welcomes it to some degree recognizes that even though he or she may do everything necessary to operate and promote the business success-fully, there are still elements he or she will be unable to control, like economic down-turns and fickle weather. A person who can tolerate risk accepts this as a normal part of doing business and proceeds accordingly.

What's your tolerance for risk? Find out by answering the following questions:

✦ Have you ever run a business of your own before? If so, how did you react when things slowed down? If you don't have experience running a business, how do you think you would react—with panic or by constantly keeping the big picture in mind?

+ How would you react if you or a family member had to spend a week in the hospital and you didn't have health insurance because you needed the money to pay the mortgage?

+ How important is it to you to have material items to validate your self-worth? What would you do if you were to suddenly lose them?

People who don't have a high tolerance for risk often see the world in black and white. Sure, the prospect of quitting your job or cutting back to part-time so that you can start your business is frightening, even to people who like some excitement. There's no safety net. What makes you think you can pull this off? What if you fail? If you're able to see these as challenges and if you like the absence of a schedule—as well as not knowing what the next day or week will bring—you should be able to deal well with the unpredictable nature that is an inevitable part of starting and running any business.

The Skills You'll Need

CERTAINLY AS an entrepreneur involved in the publishing industry,
you must have the ability to communicate clearly and convincingly to potential customers. If you know that you're lacking in certain areas, it's important that you find someone who can take over the reins that you prefer not to handle for you or to serve as a spokesperson. Though many entrepreneurs resist this from the outset, others embrace it so that they can concentrate on running and growing their business to the level they desire.

After years of experience running my own home-based publishing business, I can tell you that the most important skill you can have is the ability to keep focused on the seemingly endless details involved in keeping customers happy and coming back and generating new ideas, while working toward your long-term goals. This is not easy, and indeed, there are many times when I find myself veering off too far in one direction, spending a few days thinking about how I'm going to add 100 more active buyers to my line of greeting cards in the next six months with nary a thought about the book that I've already told my distributor that I'm planning to publish next season. If you're a born juggler, you'll probably find yourself in a similar situation from time to time. Because stuffing envelopes and performing other menial tasks gives you a break from pursuing new business and making sure that a project is completed to a customer's—and your own—satisfaction, you may sometimes find yourself doing *too* much grunt work. The opposite may happen, too—you may find you're spending too much time trying to win over new accounts and neglecting your current client roster.

Other skills that you'll need fall under the category of running a business, which I cover in Section 3. You'll need to learn about cash flow, bookkeeping, and marketing, but you can usually learn as you go and by asking other entrepreneurs from a variety of fields what business methods have worked best for them.

Even if you've never run a business before, you probably already know what you're good at from working for other people. Where your skills aren't as good, you'll be able to learn enough to get by. If you can afford to hire someone else to do some of the work, however, go ahead.

The Kind of Attitude You'll Need

IN MY eyes, the ideal home-based publishing entrepreneur is someone who's a cynical optimist (or an optimistic cynic). This is a person who has a positive attitude toward the world but who also is not terribly surprised when things go wrong. When that happens, he or she springs into action and does whatever it takes to address the problem and get everything back to normal—until the next time something turns into an emergency, that is.

As a home-based publishing entrepreneur, you'll be dealing with a variety of people and situations as well as a business, that is, in essence, operating 24 hours a day—at least in your mind. As a result, surprises will come up from time to time, especially in the beginning. As long as you maintain a positive attitude and remain alert to problems that need your immediate attention while learning which can wait, you'll be able to keep your business running while you maintain your equilibrium. Remember, at least once a week you should take a few hours to get away from the business, especially if you work from a home office; this will help you maintain your positive attitude as well.

Perhaps the most important aspect of your attitude is a firm fixation on your field, a strong sense of who your customers are and what they need, and an optimistic belief in your subject. This, more than any other part of your personality, will help you when you're dealing with current and potential customers, and provide a heavy dose of motivation to pull you through any lulls you may experience in your business.

Your Assets and Liabilities

BEFORE YOU start your home-based publishing business, it's a good idea to analyze your assets and liabilities—personal, financial, and those that involve your house, since you're going to be working from home.

As I've already mentioned, starting any business is rough. If you want to find out how you're doing, you'll have to ask someone. Unsolicited feedback will usually come from customers who are familiar with your business, but only in a trickle. If you want feedback before that, you will probably have to ask for it. Why not call some of your customers and potential customers and ask what they need, what they have no use for, and what they'd like to see that no one is currently providing?

Living where you work can also present a strain. People who run all types of home-based businesses and who are frequently overwhelmed by the workload find that one solution is to close the door to their office to take a break. Nevertheless, a home-based business will affect your entire family. How will you and your family cope with the adjustment? If you have good communication in your family and plan in advance to share some private downtime together each day, this is a definite asset and will help keep your goals about running a business in the forefront with your priorities in an order that makes sense for you.

As for money, experts always say you should budget at least twice as much as you think you need. By the way, the same philosophy applies to the amount of time you'll need to get your business up and running. But in terms of money, you'll need a financial cushion of several thousand dollars to cover both unexpected business and personal expenses at the very least, and financial experts usually recommend much more than this figure. There are always extra expenses that come up that you hadn't budgeted for, and some emergencies will come up that require an immediate infusion of cash, like renting a booth at a trade show that had slipped your mind or a special deal on an ad in a trade publication. The important thing to know is that your liabilities can be addressed quickly if you have the assets—that is, the extra cash—to fix them as soon as possible.

How Your Lifestyle Will Change

YOU MIGHT as well know in advance that once you start running your own home-based publishing business, life as you know it now will cease to exist. One comment that I hear from home-based publishing entrepreneurs of all ages is that most tasks take twice as long as they think they will, from training an employee to working on a new promotional story, to waiting for the responses to your direct mail offer to start rolling in. If you're an impatient person to begin with—like me—these delays will occasionally make you crazy and unhappy with your business. In the beginning, *everything* takes longer to get off the ground than you think, whether it's fine-tuning the content and design of your first ads or setting up your new phone system.

My advice is to dig in your heels, because your lifestyle will eventually turn around for the better.

Many home-based entrepreneurs start their businesses on a part-time basis while they're still holding down a full-time job. Consider this a warning: If you've never worked at home or for yourself before, be prepared for the business to spill over into every corner of your life, if you let it. That's why it's a good idea to take a break at least once a day and ignore the business at least one full day a week, even if your natural inclination is to work around the clock.

You may be all gung-ho about starting your own home-based publishing business, but you should take some time to consider how being an entrepreneur may affect your romantic relationships as well as your ties with friends and family, and how your friends and family might feel about your lack of time and focus toward them. You should be sure that your partner and family are in total agreement with your plans. While it's true that you may be doing most of the work of running your business, the fact is that you may need to ask friends and family to pitch in every so often to help with stuffing envelopes and proofreading copy and tolerate your absence, both physical and mental. Make sure that they understand that you're running the business for the benefit of your entire family. Even if one person in your household is opposed to the idea, you should work out your differences before you start your business. Before you proceed with your plans, be sure that you sit down with everybody that you're close to in order to get their feedback as well as serve as a sounding board for future ideas you have for the business.

PART TWO

Your Publishing Choices

Booklets

✦

Description of Business: A company that produces short-run booklets, usually containing fewer than seventy-two pages.

Ease of Startup: Easy: It's possible to write, print, and physically create the booklet at home as the orders come in.

Range of Initial Investment: If you already have a computer and desktop publishing system, you can get started for a few hundred dollars.

Time Commitment: Part-time.

Success Potential: Moderate. It's important to write compelling text for your booklets and be able to give lots of concrete information, because that is what people expect from a booklet.

How to Market the Business: Target individuals and groups who would be interested in the topic of your booklet, sell at book and craft fairs, and promote your booklets through the media.

The Pros: You're viewed as an expert on your topic.

The Cons: It's sometimes hard to get potential buyers to take you seriously because you have a booklet and not a book.

Special Considerations: If you're kicking around an idea for a book but don't want to invest the time and money that publishing a book requires, you can test your idea by publishing a booklet as a teaser.

The first thing that most people think of when they hear the word *publishing* is *books*. I think that's a shame. The truth is, the cheapest and quickest way to get into publishing is by publishing booklets.

These small, helpful publications can be written and typeset on a standard desktop system and brought to your local copy shop to be bound with a simple cover. Even though you probably won't find them in a Barnes & Noble, most booklets offer specific information designed to help readers solve a particular problem, with such titles as *50 Recipes for Busy Working Moms, Easy Tips for Training Your New Puppy*, or *Simple Accounting for Small Businesses*. The writing in booklets needn't be fancy; in fact, it's discouraged. Booklets tend to have fewer than 50 pages to keep the design simple and the costs manageable, so there simply isn't space for superfluous writing. Instead, no-nonsense writing and lots of tips and advice are what work well in booklets.

Some people who are already running their businesses frequently publish a booklet to hand out to their clients free of charge; these entrepreneurs consider booklets a way of promoting their existing businesses. Management consultants and marketing experts are often asked to

present their philosophies and policies for their clients; the easiest way to accomplish this is with a booklet.

Of course, if you have a good idea and lots of advice that can help people, you don't have to be a consultant to produce a booklet that sells and sells. No one knows this better than Paulette Ensign, who started her home-based publishing business, Organizing Solutions, with a simple idea, no money, and lots of determination. I'll let her tell her story herself:

Profile
Paulette Ensign
Organizing Solutions, Inc.
San Diego, CA

Way back in 1991, when my organizing business was already eight years old, I spotted an offer for a free copy of a booklet called *117 Ideas for Better Business Presentations*. Well, because I do business presentations and because the price was right, I sent for it. When it came, my first reaction was "I could knock out something like this about organizing tips." Then I threw it in a drawer.

Six months later I was sitting in my office, bored, baffled, and beaten down by the difficulty of selling my consulting services and workshops. I had no money. I mean *no* money! It was then that I remembered that little booklet. I had no idea how I was going to do it, but something hit me, and I knew I had to produce a booklet on organizing tips.

I started dumping all the ideas I ever had about getting organized into a file on my computer. These were all pearls that came out of my mouth when I was with clients or when I did speaking engagements or seminars. I decided I could do one booklet on business organizing tips and another on household organizing tips—two 16-page tips booklets, each fitting into a #10 envelope. The first one was *110 Ideas for Organizing Your Business Life,* and the second one was *111 Ideas for Organizing Your Household.*

My first print run was 250 copies and cost $300. That was the most expensive per-unit run I ever made, but I had to get samples to distribute to start making money. It took me a few months to pay the printer in full.

I had no money to advertise. The only way I could think of selling the booklets was by sending a copy to magazines and newspapers, asking them to use excerpts and put an invitation at the bottom for readers to send $3 plus a self-addressed stamped envelope. Some publications actually followed through.

Then the orders started dribbling in—envelopes with $3 checks in them or three $1 bills. This was great stuff. I remember the day the first one arrived. It was like manna from heaven: $3! Of course, the fact that it took about six months from first starting to write the booklets until the first $3 arrived somehow didn't matter at that moment.

I cast seeds all over the place, hoping that some would sprout. I found directories of publications at the library and started building my list. Finally, in February of 1992, the big one hit. A 12-page biweekly newsletter with 1.6 million readers ran nine lines of copy about my booklet. They didn't even use excerpts! That article sold 5,000 copies of my booklet. I distinctly remember the day I went to my P.O. box and found a little yellow slip. It said, "See clerk." A *tub* of envelopes had arrived that day, about 250 envelopes, as I recall—all with $3 in them.

In April, that same biweekly newsletter ran a similar nine lines about my household booklet, and it started all over again. This time I sold 3,000 copies.

'Round about June, I stopped and assessed what had happened. Was I making any money? By then, I had sold about 15,000 copies of the two organizing tips booklets, one copy at a time for $3. When I checked my financial records, I realized I had *not* generated a ton of money.

And some of the lessons I had learned along the way were expensive ones. I didn't realize my bank was charging me 12 cents for each item deposited until I got my first bank statement with a service charge of $191.

But some very wonderful things happened while selling those 15,000 copies. A public seminar company ordered a review copy to consider building another product from my booklet. As a result, I recorded an audio program based on my booklet. And I could sell that tape to my clients as well! In addition, it led to a 20-minute interview on a major airline's in-flight audio program during November and December one year.

As I was sorting through the envelopes I noticed a check for $1,000. It turns out a manufacturer's rep decided to send my booklets to his customers that year instead of an imprinted calendar.

A company asked me to write a booklet that was more specific to

their product line. I got speaking engagements from people who bought the booklet. I found out that the list of people who bought my booklet was a salable product.

Things were starting to pick up. But let's go back to June, when I was taking stock of my situation. You know those advertising card decks in the mail? Well, I was so bored one day, I opened one. Glancing through it, I thought to myself, "Gee, here's a company that ought to see my booklet. And here's another one, and another one." I sent booklets to each.

Less than a week later, a woman called. At first, it sounded like a prospecting call. Fortunately, I wasn't too abrupt with her. She was calling to ask me for the cost of producing 5,000 customized copies of my booklet for an upcoming trade show. She wanted to know if I could match a certain price.

I slightly underbid her price, so she was thrilled, and we agreed to the deal. I thought, "Ooh, this will be easy to sell large quantities now." Wrong. It was another three to four months until the next large-quantity sale. The organization hosting the trade show had previously rejected my booklet because I wasn't in their industry.

Now my buyer had bought 5,000 copies of my booklet, with my company information in it, to distribute at that trade show. I loved it!

One day, a guy I know from a major consumer mail-order catalog company said, "Why don't you license us reprint rights to your booklet. We can print it cheaper than you, so if you charged us a few cents a unit, you wouldn't have to do production." Well, 18 months later, after lots of zigging and zagging, that sale happened: a nonexclusive agreement for them to print 250,000 copies. We exchanged a ten-page contract for a five-digit check. They provided the booklet free with any purchase in one issue of their catalog and had a 13 percent increase in sales for that issue. They were happy. I was happy. I looked for other licensing prospects (even though it took 18 months for this sale to happen, and the five-digit check was in the low five digits, not enough to sustain me).

Around spring of 1993, I designed a class on how to write and market booklets, and wrote an 80-page manual. The class was small and mostly made up of people I knew. They paid me a fee, and I had a chance to test-run the class. So now I had another new product: an 80-page manual, a blueprint of how I had sold more than 50,000 copies of my booklet without spending a penny on advertising.

I like teaching, so now I had a new topic besides the organizing seminar I had been presenting. I also like traveling. I took the three-hour class on the road and had great fun doing it. I toured the country for about two years, teaching six to eight classes a year. I found many people who had written interesting booklets on all kinds of topics. Some have hired me to write a customized marketing plan for their booklets or to coach them by phone to develop their booklet businesses.

Midway through that year (August 1994), I discovered CompuServe. My sole purpose for getting online was to market my business. The third day I was online, I saw a forum message from a guy in Italy who had a marketing company there. He told me his client base was small businesses and companies who served small businesses. I told him I had a booklet he might find useful. I sent it to him, he liked it, and we struck a deal. He translated, produced, and marketed it, and then paid me royalties on all sales. In January 1997 he wired several thousand dollars to my checking account. He made the first sale of 105,000 copies to a magazine that bundled a copy of my booklet with one issue of their publication.

That meant I had sold more than 400,000 copies of my booklet, in two languages, without spending a penny on advertising.

One slow week, I posted a message on some CompuServe forums about the story of the Italian booklet as an example of an online success story. Even though blatant selling is not allowed on forums, creating mutually beneficial relationships is. I had received money from someone I had never spoken to and had only communicated online, by fax, by earth mail, and through electronic funds transfer, so that made it relevant for discussion.

Some folks who read those postings replied that they would be interested in doing the same thing with my booklet, but in French and in Japanese. This had never even dawned on me. I now have discussions open with people in ten different countries; within 3.5 years, this has grown into a $250,000 business. Once these relationships are established, it

makes sense to discuss brokering some other booklets, like those written by people in my classes or by people I've coached, or by those who have bought my publishing manual.

I've also discovered other opportunities for my booklet content in other formats.

+ Two different companies who produce laminated guides (one hinged, the other spiral bound) licensed my content and launched these in 1998. (They are also interested in other content, so I expect to broker the content of other booklet writers.)
+ An in-flight video information service is interested in expanding their content and is looking at my proposal.
+ I've created a new division in my company called Tips Products International.
+ I've started writing tips for booklet production and other uses by developing three different packages of 25 to 100 tips with recommended uses. These tips packages are created from the clients' materials recycled into tips or by doing original research for them.

✦ I write customized marketing plans for other people's booklets.

At the beginning of this business, I never could have written a business plan for how this has all unfolded. It arose naturally out of the continuing promotion I did for the booklets.

CHAPTER FOUR

Books

◆

Description of Business: A company that publishes a small number of books—sometimes fewer than one each year—usually on related subjects, which becomes a niche within a niche.

Ease of Startup: Difficult. You need equipment to process words and typeset, a trustworthy printing company, a talented cover and page designer, a good topic, and lively writing.

Range of Initial Investment: $10,000 for your first title; usually less for subsequent titles.

Time Commitment: Part-time to write and produce the books; full-time to market.

Success Potential: Moderate. The more people you know, and the more outgoing you are, the better your chances for success. If you can be persuasive in a lot of different situations, you can do quite well.

How to Market the Business: Through publicity, bookstores, specialty shops, even at flea markets, or with groups that have a special interest in the subjects of your books. A growing market is to sell books in bulk to companies that will use them as premiums to enhance their own image.

The Pros: There's a book in everyone; publishing it yourself will ensure it gets out.

The Cons: It's expensive to publish a book. Plus, with the tens of thousands of new books published each year, you have to be loud and/or different in order to be heard.

Special Considerations: Contrary to what you may think, bookstores may constitute a very small percentage of your sales.

"Everyone has a book inside of them." "Don't judge a book by its cover." These and countless other clichés that cite books are proof positive that our society is still in thrall with the published book. In 1998, an estimated 80,000 books were published, for all types of people and on all subjects imaginable. Put in more concrete terms, for every single day of that year, 165 new books were introduced to the market, all looking for readers. Combined with another frequently cited statistic that more than half of Americans don't buy even one book over the course of the year, some publishing entrepreneurs might read these figures and become disheartened.

However, the news is actually quite good for new book publishers. The big New York publishers still concentrate on finding and publishing the next Stephen King or the next guide to catching a man (after the runaway success of the book *The Rules*), and on these grounds, small publishers simply do not have the resources to compete effectively. But the niche markets are left wide open to the small publishers, who target markets that would seem microscopic to the big guys. Say you have an idea for a book on how to start a floral business because, after all, that's how you've spent the last 15 years of your life. Great. You're an expert. If you sell a couple thousand copies a year, you'll be a success. To a publisher the size of Random House or Simon & Schuster, 2,000 copies sold is a failure.

In fact, many small book publishers that specialize in niche markets today know that their books are unlikely to ever see the inside of a bookstore. Marketing directly to your likely customers through publicity, direct mail, and other means will not only net you more money than bookstore distribution, but you also have the advantage of building a list of your customers, which will be quite valuable if you choose to expand your publishing empire; after all, if they bought a book on the floral business, they might also buy an audiotape, subscribe to a newsletter, and attend a seminar on the same subject.

Profile
Jim Hoskins
Maximum Press
Gulf Breeze, Florida

One of the fastest growing topics for publishers of any type is computers: how to use them, how to program them, and even how to use them to market your business.

Jim Hoskins started his company, Maximum Press, with this in mind.

Hoskins has been involved in the computer and high-tech fields from its earliest days. He worked at IBM for ten years and had a degree in electrical engineering. While still at IBM, Hoskins wrote a book about a product he was developing, and the book was eventually published by John Wiley & Sons, a large business publisher in New York. He wrote a few other books about IBM products while still an employee, and he transferred within the company to Gulf Breeze, Florida, where he took a marketing job. This is where he began to contemplate his future:

> I was trying to figure out what to do, because at that point, I was on the management fast track to become an executive at IBM. So I took a poll and asked other executives if they would follow the same path if they had it to do over again. They all said no because they moved a lot, worked too much, and never saw their families.

Hoskins took a look at the books he wrote and saw them as alternatives to the gerbil-wheel lifestyle at IBM. He then took a one-year leave of absence from the company to write full-time and start his own publishing company specializing in computer books. Six months into his leave of absence, IBM offered an incentive plan to employees to quit during one of its early downsizing waves. Hoskins accepted the offer. That was in 1992. In January of 1993, he incorporated as Maximum Press and started his publishing company, with IBM as his first client. He could have concentrated on writing books, but he saw that he could make more money on the publishing side than on the writing side.

That first year, at the age of 34, Hoskins published three books. The first was about a software package that IBM had produced for the manufacturing world. "I made IBM commit up front to the number of books they would buy, and I made sure that their commitment alone was enough to make the book profitable," says Hoskins. For awhile, he thought he would only publish books that relied on these deals with IBM so that he could build up some cash to publish the books he really wanted to do. Since the books were only of interest to IBM, Hoskins couldn't begin to think about bookstore distribution.

But once he had enough cash to publish books for consumers, which obviously provided him with a larger audience than just IBM, Hoskins began to plan these books and pursue bookstore distribution. In 1994, he signed up with Publishers Group West, a major distributor for small publishers, which gave him access to a whole new market. He was able to broaden the subjects of his company's titles just based on the distribution.

His first consumer-oriented title, *Marketing on the Internet*, has sold 12,000 copies in a year. Future books will include an Internet shopping guide and other consumer-oriented titles that will sell well through bookstore distribution as well as in other markets.

By 1998, Hoskins was publishing eight to ten new books each year in two distinct markets: one directed at IBM and trade, the other directed away from IBM completely. Since he began his company, Hoskins has worked out of his home office, though it hasn't always been easy. He converted a spare bedroom into an office. From the beginning, he has always had at least one employee to "take care of the things that I didn't want to do myself," which included bookkeeping. He had the room remodeled to look like a regular office and bought office furniture and a professional phone system. It worked for awhile, but in time, Hoskins started to dislike having an employee traipse in and out of his house during the day. So he solved the problem by building a 750-square-foot office suite onto his home with enough room to accommodate up to three employees. More importantly, this office has its own separate entrance, so Hoskins feels his work life doesn't interfere with his personal life.

As it turned out, Hoskins's first employee was embezzling from the business by forging checks, so Hoskins fired

him and got the money back. "It was troubling to have someone you're trying to nurture take advantage of you like that," he says, and he has learned to be more careful when hiring employees.

Hoskins serves as the publisher and editor at Maximum Press; other people handle finance and administration, management, customer service, and marketing and publicity. He farms out the production work on his books to a local subcontractor and intends to grow the company by using subcontractors or employees where appropriate:

I tried subcontracting the company's marketing efforts, but that didn't work because the database for this branch needed to be available to everyone in the office. I also wanted to be able to oversee the development of the marketing database so it could be done correctly. But even if we become as big as Microsoft, I still intend to work out of my home office and have satellite offices for the overflow.

Hoskins hasn't noticed that his youth has affected his ability to run his business or the willingness of others to work with him. "Being younger and weaned on computers, I might be more willing to exploit technology than someone who's 50 and just starting a business," he says. "But then again, I have a friend who told me his grandmother refused to talk on the phone because she didn't like to talk into a box. Change comes hard to some people. Younger entrepreneurs have an advantage that way."

What surprises Hoskins the most about being an entrepreneur is the sheer volume of opportunities he has to choose from. "Knowing that my choices are going to make the difference between life and death, I want to do them all, but I don't want to spend my life doing them all," he says. "I *could* do more than I am right now, but I don't want to work 80 hours a week.

"*Nothing* is more valuable than your time," he continues. "If you make a lot of money and have a successful business but have no time left over, you lose. The ideal mix is to have a business selling products and information, but not time, because time is more valuable than money. I can launch products and they'll live their own little lives while I'm not working. But if I'm a dentist, if I'm not working, I'm not making money."

Hoskins believes that by running an information business from his home, he has a degree of flexibility that others only dream of. "If I take a day off, I know it's not directly affecting my income," he says. He also has a seven-year-old son and triplets who are still in diapers. In addition to running the business and watching his kids, Hoskins goes for an hour bike ride each day. He considers the ride to be part of his work day because he brings a tape recorder with him and says he thinks of many ideas during that hour.

Coming from the corporate world, I know how hard corporate jobs can be on families and I don't think that it's healthy or good in the long term for either the country or for society. I don't think that businesses will be able to continue long term in that vein. The people who work for me are mothers, and whenever their children are sick, there's never any question of whether they have to come in to work that day. If there's a class party, they can leave in the middle of the day. Their children come here after school and do homework, and play with my children sometimes. There are a lot of people who are not in the workforce who can't justify wrecking their families for the sake of a job. I'm happy that I'm able to give them an option by working here, and they just love it. I don't pay huge salaries, but because I have a family orientation I'm going to be able to get good employees at bargain prices. After all, I'm helping to support their families.

His advice to other people who want to start a home-based publishing business is to go slowly and save as much money as you can before you start. He recommends that you use that time to plan and think. "Pick a publishing niche business that positions your lifestyle the way you want it to be," he advises.

Greeting Cards

✦

Description of Business: A company that produces greeting cards and other stationery products, such as notepaper, wrapping paper, and ribbon.

Ease of Startup: Moderate. If you start on a small-scale basis, you'll have less money tied up in inventory, but it will take longer to get established since many retailers and others in the distribution channel won't take you seriously if you carry fewer than 80 different cards.

Range of Initial Investment: To start with a line of 20 different cards, $5,000. To start with 100 cards, promotional catalogs, rack display cards, and other retailer tools, $25,000 and up.

Time Commitment: Full-time, especially if you choose to sell direct to consumers and to the wholesale market.

Success Potential: Moderate. If you have your eye on widespread wholesale distribution, be aware that it may take years to build up to that point. In the meantime, developing a following with your own customers can convince distributors and retailers to stock your cards. As always, focusing on a particular market will help.

How to Market the Business: By servicing your sales reps promptly and attentively, providing attractive deals to retailers, exhibiting at trade shows for the gift trade, and producing catalogs that advertise an ever-changing line of new cards and other stationery products.

The Pros: It's a fun business, and you're helping people to express their feelings.

The Cons: It's a lot harder than it looks. Greeting cards are very fragile objects and can get damaged during shipping and in a display rack. Retail accounts require the option of returning unsold seasonal cards after a holiday is over.

Special Considerations: Study the market and try to make your cards different from everything else out there.

The greeting card business is fun, but highly competitive. It can be extremely lucrative, however, if you hit the industry just right. Here are the facts about the industry, as provided by the Greeting Card Association, based in Washington, DC.

✦ Approximately 7.4 billion greeting cards are purchased annually by American consumers, generating roughly $6.3 billion in U.S. retail sales.

✦ Of the total greeting cards purchased annually, roughly half are seasonal and the remaining half are everyday cards. Sales of everyday cards, especially nonoccasion cards, are on the increase.

✦ The most popular card-sending holidays are, in order, Christmas, Valentine's Day, Easter, Mother's Day, and Father's Day.

✦ People of all ages and types exchange greeting cards. Women purchase approximately 85 percent of all greeting cards; the average card purchaser is a woman in her middle years, although this demographic picture may be changing.

✦ Cards range in price from 35¢ to $10.00, with the average card retailing for around $1.50. Cards featuring special techniques and new technologies are at the top of this price scale.

✦ The average person receives 30 cards per year, eight of which are birthday cards.

✦ Estimates indicate that there are around 1,500 greeting card publishers in America, ranging from major corporations to small family organizations. Greeting Card Association members together account for approximately 90 percent of the industry market share.

The greeting card industry is as varied as the thousands of individuals who are pursuing the field. Many people who enter the field are artists who want to circulate their paintings, drawings, and photographs beyond their own studios. It's inexpensive to put together a portfolio of

10 to 20 greeting cards, and so many people have traveled down this road.

However, because it's so easy to get started in the greeting card business—and much more difficult to maintain business and grow beyond the common initial venues of local stores and craft fairs—retailers see an awful lot of unprofessionally produced cards, which may explain the lukewarm reception that many novice greeting card producers get when they first enter the market.

Admittedly, as I write this, I'm only in my first year of running a greeting card business, and that in an extremely small niche. However, I have learned much about what to focus on and what to avoid in the course of selling my greeting cards. So here goes.

Profile
Lisa Shaw
Litterature
Grafton, New Hampshire

As is the case with every other kind of publishing business I've run in the course of 15 years, I've never been good at taking my own advice. I always come up with the idea first, do a little research, and then plunge right in. This is what happened when I decided to start a greeting card company.

Being a slave to a number of cats—currently six—and having authored two books about cats for other book publishers, I had always had my eye out for a publishing business I could start that involved cats, and dogs as well. It wasn't until the holiday season of 1994 that lightning struck.

My husband Dan and I were playing with the two cats we had at the time, Margo and Squiggy, when suddenly Dan said he thought it was a shame that the cats hadn't received any Christmas cards. We started to think about all of the different occasions when it would be nice to send a greeting card to a cat or dog—or to receive one from them. We filled several sheets of paper with ideas and then decided to start a company making cards for pets—they could send these cards to you and to each other, or you could use them to convey news about your pets to your friends.

My next decision was what to use as art for the front of the cards. I had worked with a cartoonist on a humor book about pigs and I thought his style would work well. I told him about my idea and he sent a few rough sketches, but I decided I shouldn't use him: What if he decided to bail out after the first line of cards? I wanted a consistent look to the cards and didn't want to have to rely on one artist.

At the time, I was dealing in antiques and collecting antique postcards of my town. One day, I was leafing through the Grafton postcards at a local antique mall when I noticed a file card a few rows over for cat postcards. I liked what I saw and spent the next three months buying up postcards with cats, and later dogs, after several friends told me of many occasions when they had altered a human card to give to their dogs. The big advantage to using these original postcards is that they were essentially copyright-free: They were produced in the 1890s and early 1900s, and the companies that owned them went out of business around World War I. So I didn't have to pay anyone to use these illustrations, and the pictures were absolutely charming and very different from any other greeting cards that I had seen on the market.

My next step was to come up with the various categories of cards. I went to a few of the cat- and dog-specific Internet mailing lists and groups and asked people to tell me about occasions when they had sent a card to a cat or dog. I came up with 14 categories for each, including adoption announcements, holiday cards, get well cards, cards to say thanks to the vet and groomer, and sympathy cards.

I had originally thought to produce only 40 cards in my first line. However, once I included dogs, I decided to go for broke (literally!) and produce 100 cards.

One long day, I took my 900 postcards and started to match them up with specific categories: for instance, one postcard worked better as a humorous card, while another was great for a vet appointment reminder card. Then I had to be

equitable: If I had a happy birthday card for a cat, I also had to have one for a dog. There were occasions I had thought of, but had no card to match, so I went back to the antique malls and postcard shows.

Later I found a graphic designer who scanned the postcards into his desktop publishing program, cleaned up the imperfections, and laid them out for the printer, including some verse on the inside of the card and the identifying information, such as including a Universal Product Code (UPC) or bar code—on the back. Most retailers and all of the chains require UPCs on every product they sell. He also helped to design the 28-page catalog I would use to solicit consumers and retailers.

Once we were done with the cards and catalogs, it was time to design the display cards for the racks that would tell the buyer whether a card was a dog adoption card or a cat sympathy card. Plus I decided to produce both horizontal and vertical cards, so this meant that we needed at least 56 different types of rack cards: 14 categories, one horizontal, one vertical, for both cats and dogs.

The display cards that are placed in a holder above the rack—called *toppers*—were simple; just our company name, a brief description, and our logo.

Once everything was at the printer, it was time to find some suppliers, such as the company that would supply me with greeting card racks. I later learned that most wholesale orders tend to be for individual cards in quantities of one dozen each, and not for rack plans, since many retailers either already own the racks or will place the cards in a long floor rack model, not the spinning display racks that I think display the cards at their best.

I designed the wholesale order form for Litterature with a simple spreadsheet program, allowing one line for each card; each line contains the unit number that I've assigned it plus a brief description of the card.

I also decided to go for broke and develop a few gift packages that my customers might be interested in. I had heard about people throwing birthday parties for their cats and dogs, and so I designed a party kit that contained party invitations (our own, of course!), some toys and treats, and party favors for guests to bring home to their own pets. Also included was a mug with our logo on it, along with some catnip or dog biscuits, which means that whenever an order comes in, we always ask, "Is that for a cat or a dog?"

One additional design we used for the cards included paw prints on both sides of the envelope, along with a very tiny version of our logo and the Litterature name. We had to follow certain postal regulations, but I thought it added a nice touch.

The fateful day came when the cards were ready to be picked up from the printer. Since I knew I was going to market the cards to consumers, I had drawn

up a press kit (see Chapter 16) and developed a mailing list of about 500 media people.

My first press mailing resulted in some media attention and lots of requests for free catalogs. I brought these newspaper articles—from the *San Francisco Chronicle*, *Boston Globe*, and the *Wall Street Journal*—with me to a couple of pet industry trade shows, where I exhibited the cards. I made some contacts with wholesale accounts, sold some cards, and met sales reps who were interested in selling the cards. I also met a magazine editor who later wrote a story about the cards, which resulted in some business.

The next step was to pursue wholesale accounts more aggressively. Armed with the positive media reviews, I bought a directory of sales reps who sold to the gift trade and sent each a catalog, sample card, order form, and press clips. From this first round, I signed up 50 sales reps located all over the country.

Roughly six months after I began the business, I can say that I've learned a lot about the greeting card business and know that I still have a lot more to learn. It's a lot like other forms of publishing, but it's also different because I couldn't simply sell the cards to consumers. I had to sell to wholesale accounts, an entirely different game than selling directly to consumers.

Unlike the newsletters I published and edited, greeting cards are created once, then marketed continually.

Response from consumers has been pretty low because people just aren't accustomed to ordering individual greeting cards out of a catalog. Usually, they go into a gift shop, select a gift, then wander over to the greeting card department. It's frequently difficult to teach people a new way of doing things, even if it's more convenient for them.

So, as any good home-based publishing entrepreneur should do, I've decided to branch out. In addition to the cards, I've sold a number of birthday party kits, personalized Christmas stockings, and writing kits for cats and dogs (a rubber stamp paw print, an ink pad, and a selection of greeting cards). I'm going to continue to introduce new gift items for pets: The latest are gift baskets to celebrate a special day in your dog or cat's life, a dog bath basket, and sympathy baskets to be sent to a person who's just lost a cat or dog.

I'll continue to market to both consumers and wholesale markets. Whenever Litterature is written up in a consumer publication, I'll inevitably receive calls from bookstores, pet stores, and gift shops that are interested in carrying the cards.

As with all of the home-based publishing businesses I've run, I've mostly learned as I've gone along. As some ideas and marketing methods don't pan out, I scrap them and look for more.

One thing I have learned is never to say no. You never know who's watching and whether a small sale to a consumer will lead to a huge order from a chain store. That's what keeps me going, along with the fact that I never stop learning about the business.

Magazines

✦

Description of Business: A company that publishes a magazine on a specific topic, appearing anywhere from biweekly to quarterly.

Ease of Startup: Moderate. If you have a desktop computer system, you can write, lay out, and print an issue in a short period of time. Distribution—free or paid—frequently requires outside help.

Range of Initial Investment: $3,000 and up.

Time Commitment: Full-time. Many publishers focus on editorial and production, hiring an outside sales staff for advertising.

Success Potential: Difficult. Many magazines are unable to draw the amount of advertising and/or subscribers necessary to cover costs.

How to Market the Business: With sufficient distribution, trades with radio stations, promotional and event tie-ins with other businesses, and a quality publication.

The Pros: You're viewed as a voice of the community.

The Cons: Hard work. Collecting money from advertisers.

Special Considerations: In the last decade, magazines have become more narrow. Find a topic and an audience that's not being addressed.

Ah, the wonderful world of magazines. In the old days, *Saturday Review* and *Reader's Digest* reigned. Today, it's *Snowshoe Quarterly*, *My Ferret*, and *Dental Hygienist Leisure Time*, which shows you how far people have taken the idea of niche publishing.

Magazine publishing—four-color, glossy, with lots of ads—is perhaps the most difficult and time-consuming type of publishing. It's almost impossible to run it as a one-person business, because advertising, newsstand distribution, editorial, design, and circulation are each labor-intensive in and of themselves, not to mention the financial end of things. This is true even for very small magazines. A woman I know who published a beautiful four-color magazine to publicize the town of Woodstock, Vermont, had a veritable force of warm bodies helping her meet quarterly deadlines.

Four out of every five new magazines will fail by their second birthday. Don't be afraid to start small, but be sure to create a demand from your readers, which will, in turn, create a demand from advertisers who want to reach them. If you haven't already penned a few freelance articles for some small or regional magazines, then get moving. Writing an article for a particular publication will give you an idea how to slant a story toward a particular type of reader, which you can then extrapolate into creating an entire magazine. By the way, a great beginning exercise for your proposed magazine is to describe your reader in 25 words, then draw up a sample table of contents for your first six issues.

Profile
Gloria Bursey
***Choices* Magazine**
Grand Rapids, Michigan

When Gloria Bursey decided to stop publishing a regional women's magazine called *Glory*, she told herself she never wanted to publish another magazine as long as she lived. Then she became a widow and had no choice but to start looking for work. "I was known as a writer in this area, but no one wanted to hire me," she remembers. "It seems they would rather hire somebody younger, to whom they didn't have to pay as much money."

At the same time she looked around for advice about retirement and aging issues, but didn't have much luck. "What I saw out there didn't tell me very much," she recalls, "and people are living longer and have much more retirement time than before." She thought about breaking her promise and starting another magazine, this time on retirement and aging.

Bursey began by talking with seniors around town to find out what they would like to see in a magazine geared toward them. She also met with prospective advertisers. She wrote up some columns and features, and designed the layout on a Macintosh computer (when she had published *Glory* she had relied on typesetters). Before she knew it, she was publishing another magazine.

Choices is a 16-page monthly newsmagazine. She prints about 23,000 copies each month and has a readership of about 40,000. Most of her sales staff of five are retired; she pays them a 23 percent commission.

Though Bursey still writes the editorial and an occasional article, she relies mainly on outside writers to fill the pages. She's never had a problem finding reliable writers, because people will write or call to suggest stories. "*Choices* has a mix of columns and features," explains Bursey. "We recently featured Ms. Senior Michigan, who's in her seventies." The magazine also includes a financial column, a travel story, a health column, and stories geared toward singles. Though she is starting to include some controversial stories in the magazine—about hospices and Medicaid—Bursey tries to keep the tone upbeat. "I think too many papers are negative," she points out.

There's also a calendar of local events and a column by a local man who's 93. Bursey pays her writers $25 for a column, $35 for a short article, and up to $125 for a long story.

Each issue is free. Bursey distributes the magazine in over 200 places within a 60-mile radius, including grocery stores, department stores, restaurants, and senior centers. Even though it's a free publication, she still strives to make the cover inviting. It started out in black and white and is now four-color.

"I started the magazine because I'm a writer," she says, but admits she was a little bit ahead of herself because businesses weren't used to gearing their advertising toward people over 50. Now they're used to the idea. The magazine has a 50/50 advertising to editorial ratio: Each page contains half ads and half editorial. In general, the smaller the publication is, the more you have to load it with advertising. "As it gets larger," Bursey points out, "you make more money and you can have more editorial."

Advertisers are billed when the issue comes out. Some take a while to pay, however, and Bursey turns some over to an attorney for collection. "Our policy is if they don't pay by the second ad, they can't place another ad until they've paid. If it's a new business, I suggest we get payment in advance."

Bursey also writes a column for a local newspaper, which she is trying to syndicate to more mainstream papers in the region. She also does some photography for the magazine, working out of her home. She's looking into the possibility of expanding *Choices* to cover the entire state of Michigan, but then she'd have to approach a completely different type of advertiser to make it fly. "I love publishing because it keeps me active in the community," reports Bursey. "I'm in the center of everything because *I'm* the media."

She thinks magazine publishing would be a great business for a couple to run, with one keeping the books and the other selling ads. "Even if you aren't a writer, you can always find people to write for you. After all it's impossible to do everything. People are aging more slowly these days—I call it *Star Trek* time, or time that we didn't think we'd have. Occasionally I meet editors who do everything on a magazine, and I don't know how they do it."

Newsletters

✦

Description of Business: A company that publishes one or more subscription newsletters that focus on a very specific field.

Ease of Startup: Moderate. You need one sample issue to start.

Range of Initial Investment: $500 if you already have a computer.

Time Commitment: Part- or full-time

Success Potential: Easy. Be sure you fill a niche that nobody else is addressing and have the marketing plan to back it up.

How to Market the Business: Through direct mail, publicity, conferences, lectures, and advertising.

The Pros: It's satisfying to have people pay for what you have to say.

The Cons: Sometimes it's difficult to get subscribers to renew.

Special Considerations: Newsletter publishing is for people who have a particular interest and are able to address it in very specific ways.

Publishing a newsletter will appeal to anyone who believes passionately enough in a particular topic to want to invest their time and money in it. It's also important that you enjoy letting other people know how you feel about your subject. Sometimes, in fact, your interest may be close to an obsession.

Unlike other publications, it's possible to be as opinionated as you want in your newsletter, and your readers will love you for it.

Even though publishing a newsletter involves a lot of hard work, the rewards are ample: instant expert status, in-depth knowledge on a particular topic, and what is effectively your own forum in each and every issue. I'll warn you now that the skills you'll develop by publishing your own newsletter, and the headiness of having your own publication, will get into your blood.

The good news is that it's both cheap—if you want it to be—and easy to start publishing a newsletter on a certain topic to sell on a subscription basis. However, after you begin, you may frequently encounter one or all of the following reactions:

+ Is that all there is?
+ Do you really expect me to pay that much money for a subscription?
+ Why don't you just publish a magazine instead of pretending that you want to be one?

Then there's the flip side of the newsletter business. Because, by its very merits, a newsletter is supposed to deliver concise information about a very narrow subject, those people who are interested in that subject frequently react with manic enthusiasm:

+ They tear open the envelope the minute they retrieve it from the mailbox, sit down on the floor, and read it right then and there, cover to cover.
+ They hoard every copy and keep them in fireproof boxes.
+ They write to the publisher and ask what they need to do to become a lifetime subscriber.

Today it's estimated that anywhere from 100,000 to 200,000 newsletters are published each year. Even I was shocked when I read these figures, but when you start to think about the wide variety of newsletters that you probably already receive—from the PTA, your church, or your dentist, or one that contains nothing but chocolate recipes, as well as the one your company publishes for its employees and stockholders four times a year—well, then, this figure begins to make sense.

Typically, a newsletter is published about a specific subject or for a particular group. As such, it may go into great detail on the subject, details that may bore the casual observer but will thrill a person who's seriously interested in the topic. A newsletter can be as brief as one page or as long as 32—and I've seen newsletters that are even longer. A newsletter may be published once a year or once a day, may be created with a typewriter or the latest in desktop publishing software, and may be run off with an old-fashioned mimeograph machine or on fancy textured paper with several colors of ink or even color photos. And it could have 20 readers or 200,000 readers.

A newsletter can also be a perfect way to impart information to members of an association who rely on it for news about the group and upcoming events. This is a different type of newsletter, one that's not sold by subscription. A business may also decide to create a promotional newsletter to inform current customers about new products or to attract new customers. Church groups and trade organizations often use newsletters to keep their members informed about news that concerns the group. Some newsletter publishers get started by offering to produce newsletters for these types of organizations, which is a great way to generate revenue and develop your publishing skills. However, since it is usually the burning desire to get your voice, opinions, and advice out there to readers, most of the information here pertains to publishing and editing a newsletter to sell by subscription.

Some people may think that you want to publish a newsletter because you can't afford or are too lazy to publish a magazine, but the truth is that the subjects of most newsletters are far too specific to warrant the expense and size of a magazine, which is supported more by its advertising revenue than by subscription fees. In addition, the majority of newsletters don't accept advertising.

A newsletter offers several advantages over a magazine, which is why there are at least ten times more newsletters than magazines. Here are just a few advantages:

✦ Since you're not supported by advertising, you don't have to worry about offending an advertiser by something you may say in the newsletter.

✦ Since newsletter production is pretty straightforward, the amount of time you spend on writing, designing, and printing it is much less than a magazine. Given this flexibility, you can add late-breaking news up to an hour before delivery to the printer or copy shop.

✦ The more specific you get in your newsletter articles, the more your readers will love it, which means you'll get to explore topics too insignificant for a larger audience. For instance, in a newsletter about model trains, an article about one of the early designers would be welcomed. In a more general magazine about hobbies, it would probably be too specific.

While subscription rates will be your main source of income, ancillary products such as special reports, seminars, books, and tapes can reap great profits. You can produce them yourself or buy them at wholesale rates from other publishers—and the more you sell the lower your cost per unit. Special reports of four to ten pages can cost about a dollar a page, audiotapes of special programs can be priced from $10 to $25, and the profit margin if you sell books by other publishers can be as high as 40 percent, as long as you charge extra for shipping and handling.

Though seminars can be a lot of work, they bring in extra income from current subscribers and attract potential customers who may buy some of your products and subscribe to your newsletter. A seminar can be anything from a 90-minute evening program held in a rented room at the local YMCA to a full-fledged, week-long convention, complete with a full roster of experts in your field who give workshops, a trade show with hundreds of exhibitors, and other special social programs for attendees.

Some seminar organizers charge an admission fee—especially when the seminar lasts a day or more—while others let people in for free in the hopes that they'll subscribe to their newsletter or sign up for a later seminar that does charge a fee. The custom is to offer a discount if an attendee signs up well in advance of the workshop, and to charge full price up to a week before the seminar begins and for admission at the door. In any case, the seminar producer doesn't expect to profit off the admission fees, but instead hopes to raise enough money to cover the cost of the room rental as well as the money spent to promote the event.

When setting prices on the products you sell, remember to be flexible, especially if expected profits don't immediately materialize. Keep in mind that in some cases—particularly newsletters for business people and investors—if you set the price too low, potential readers may be turned off because they may perceive it to have no value.

Profile
Elaine Floyd
Newsletter News & Resources
St. Louis, Missouri

Elaine Floyd was one of the pioneers in the newsletter business back in the early 1980s. She wrote and edited nonsubscription newsletters to use as sales tools. She produced her newsletters on the first Macintosh computer using the first version of PageMaker, a common desktop publishing program.

Floyd's background was in engineering, and she worked in sales and marketing for a high-tech company in Nashville. "I was driving all over the south, and I was so busy that I frequently forgot to tell my clients everything they needed to know," she says. So she started publishing a newsletter that provided her clients with the information she might have left out of her meetings. When company management saw how well the newsletter worked to increase sales in Floyd's territory, they decided to distribute it company-wide and use it as a marketing tool for a dozen salespeople. The company's art department took care of laying it out and typesetting it. However, Floyd later realized she could produce the newsletter for her company much more cheaply on a Macintosh of her own, so the company assigned her that responsibility. Once she had the equipment, she began to look for other newsletter jobs on the side. In a short time, she had a full-fledged business going, and she decided to get out of travel and sales.

Soon she was producing newsletters with four full-time employees for 25 clients, mostly from high-tech and industrial companies. Unfortunately, she found that she was spending more time managing her employees and the business and less time actually working on the newsletter. When Floyd moved to New Orleans with her husband because of his job promotion, she disbanded her business and started over from scratch.

This time Floyd was determined to keep her business small. She designed a promotional newsletter to tout her services. Although she got a few jobs, more importantly, she heard from people who wanted to subscribe to her promotional newsletter. After some hesitation, Floyd converted her newsletter into what is now *Newsletter News & Resources*, a quarterly eight-page publication for writers, designers, and entrepreneurs who are producing their own newsletters and need some guidance.

Floyd says that the biggest difference between publishing a client newsletter and a subscription newsletter is that people are paying for the information. "I have so much pressure to publish information that's valuable and fresh that it takes me so much longer to do my own newsletter than if it was strictly a marketing piece," she says.

Though she charges $19.95 for a subscription, Floyd still uses the newsletter as a promotional piece for her other products, which have grown to include several books on how to publish a newsletter to promote your own business or somebody else's and how to use the newsletter to market your business. Her first book, *Marketing with Newsletters*, has sold 13,000 copies through lectures, seminars, bookstores, and mail order. She also thinks about forming a newsletter society, in which subscribers would purchase a membership and be entitled to a subscription to *Newsletter News & Resources*, a book or two, and a directory of newsletter printers.

During her years of producing newsletters—for her own business as well as other companies—Floyd understandably has a lot of advice to give to the aspiring newsletter publisher:

Your topic has to be narrow enough so that it has PR value and you have some kind of a niche, so pick your subject carefully and make sure you know where to find your prospective buyers. Your topic also has to contain a lot of information that is constantly changing and that people have trouble finding on their own. Using my own example, if I were to publish this newsletter as my sole business, it would be tough because it's hard to find newsletter editors.

Since marketing through direct mail is very expensive, Floyd recommends that you pick a subject that subscribers won't hesitate spending money on to get the kind of information they need. The easiest way is to find a real specialized niche of a big business that has money to spend. It makes it easier on you because you don't have to go after as many subscribers. "If I could publish a newsletter that costs $199 a year, I'd need only 200 subscribers and

I'd be sitting pretty," she says. "With my newsletter, I'd have to have 2,000 subscribers to pull in the same amount of money. New technologies are a good bet for this, as well as any subject that's really hot and that people are really confused about—like the Internet."

Floyd adds that she thinks people get excited about publishing a newsletter because of the possibility of the get-rich-quick aspect. One newsletter that is regularly held up as an example is *The Tightwad Gazette*, which Floyd says is successful because it contains a lot of unusual information in each issue, it's wonderfully written, it's based on a lot of research, and you can tell that the editor Amy Daczyzyn really worked hard on it. "Plus, she's been a real PR queen," says Floyd. "But still, her success didn't happen overnight. Most people don't realize what it takes, and you have to love your subject enough to do it."

Newspapers

✦

Description of Business: A company that publishes a weekly, monthly, or quarterly newspaper that focuses on a particular community or area.

Ease of Startup: Moderate. You need to publish a sample issue to demonstrate your newspaper's focus to advertisers.

Range of Initial Investment: $500–$5,000.

Time Commitment: Full-time.

Success Potential: Moderate. This can be successful if there's no competition or if you're addressing a niche that's not being filled.

How to Market the Business: Through radio ads, event sponsorships, adequate distribution, reader contests, and other publicity.

The Pros: Publishing your own newspaper is a way to become the voice of a particular community.

The Cons: Advertisers sometimes pay late or not at all; readers will frequently cancel subscriptions for frivolous reasons.

Special Considerations: For a person with experience in journalism, publishing a newspaper is a power trip. It will get into your blood.

Producing a newspaper is not a common home-based publishing business. The very idea of producing a daily newspaper conjures up images of a noisy, smoky newsroom with harried reporters running around under deadline. But the truth is, specialized newspapers, which are geared toward a specific audience, as well as small, community-based weeklies, can be easily handled from the home. One person can handle the editorial from a home computer while another can sell ads. An independent contractor or distribution company should be hired to get the paper out to the public, whether it's free of charge or not.

If you decide to publish a newspaper, you will never have the luxury of time that some other home-based publishing entrepreneurs have, even though they would probably laugh at you if you told them this. With weekly deadlines, or even monthly deadlines, there are no such things as fact checkers or assistants. Basically the story goes into the paper the way it comes into the office, with precious little time to content edit or copy edit.

Why would you publish a newspaper instead of a newsletter or magazine? For one, newsprint is cheaper than the paper used in printing a newsletter or magazine, and printing is a faster one-feed process, which means you can work closer to deadline, which is necessary in a local, community-based weekly paper that publishes the news about the schools, senior center, and local businesses.

Profile
Chuck Woodbury
Out West
Grass Valley, California

Like many people, Chuck Woodbury didn't like his job. Unlike most people, he quit his job and used his savings to travel around the western United States in an RV for two years. During that time his most pressing decision was whether to turn left, right, or go straight at a congruence of dirt roads out in the middle of nowhere.

Woodbury had been working in public relations on a freelance basis for ten years when he decided it was time to bail out. He also published a small monthly newspaper, which he sold to finance his bare-bones living expenses for a couple of years.

Somewhere in the middle of Wyoming toward the end of the first year of traveling, Woodbury thought of combining his two passions—traveling and writing—into a business he could run himself. Woodbury published the first issue of *Out West* barely six weeks later. Today *Out West* is a quarterly, 40-page newspaper filled mostly with Woodbury's stories about the places he visits and the people he sees.

In the beginning, the paper was 24 pages and had 25 subscribers—mostly Woodbury's family and friends. After the first issue was published, he sent copies out to the press. Shortly thereafter, the news media started calling. A few months later, Woodbury appeared on ABC's *World News Tonight*, and the subscriptions started to pour in.

Despite the power they wield, many members of the media are as unhappy with their jobs as the rest of the world. Chuck feels that the media responded so enthusiastically to *Out West* because many journalists would love to do what he was doing. They naturally believed a lot of their readers would feel the same way. "I was doing something I loved. I was able to make a living from it, but went into it on a shoestring," he says. "Also, I was free. That's why the media wrote about me so much, and that's why people subscribe."

To do the research for an issue, Woodbury spends about a month on the road with his wife, Rodica—who serves as associate editor—and their young daughter, Emily. They decide to cover a certain area before they leave; they stick to the less-frequently traveled roads and avoid the interstates.

He writes and designs the newspaper on a Macintosh. On the road he uses a laptop computer, importing the data into the Macintosh when he gets home. One reason he started the newspaper was because he thought it would be fun; he has to work really hard to keep the business part of the paper under control. "I've been tempted a few times to increase the frequency of the paper to bimonthly, but then everything would become a chore," he says. "Besides, I don't want to hire anybody because then I'd be a boss. I'm more concerned about putting out a good product than spending a lot of time promoting the paper. By putting out a quality product, it promotes itself."

Woodbury still sends news releases and sample copies to the media. He does radio talk shows over the phone while he's traveling and when he's at home. "I do about four or five shows a month on big-city radio stations. I phone in from wherever I am. It's a good source of new subscriptions."

Out West accepts advertising, but Woodbury doesn't do much to solicit new ads; as a result, the ratio of editorial to advertising space is about nine to one. The paper grosses about $100,000 a year from subscriptions and ancillary products, such as a videotape and a book Woodbury wrote for a major publisher. He'd like to spend more time increasing the renewal rate, which stands at 60 percent, but he can only send out a few renewal notices. "I don't like to play that game," he indicates, but many people won't renew until they get a fifth notice, so he's added another mailing.

Woodbury writes and lays out the paper before sending it to the printer, who then passes it along to a mailing service. Woodbury maintains his own mailing list. "It's important to keep your overhead really low," he warns. "Don't get carried away with equipment, even though it's easy to become addicted to the new technology."

For people who are thinking about starting their own newspaper, Woodbury has a tip: "Find a subject that's of burning interest to you. With the new technology, it's very easy and affordable to get the word out."

Software

✦

Description of Business: A company that publishes information in a computer-readable format.

Ease of Startup: Moderate. You don't need to know how to program software; you do need a good idea and the fortitude to market it for the long term and produce updates when necessary.

Range of Initial Investment: $7,500 for programming fees for a simple program and no fancy packaging; $15,000 and up for something more substantial.

Time Commitment: Part- to full-time.

Success Potential: Moderate. Copycat programs are doomed to failure. You need to produce a program that people will use in their daily lives and that contains something different from other programs currently on the market.

How to Market the Business: Through direct mail, publicity, sales reps and wholesaling to software stores, and selling in bulk to organizations and businesses.

The Pros: In most cases, you don't need to invest money in keeping a large inventory, since the turnaround time on duplicating programs tends to be brief. Plus, you don't need to be fluent in programming to produce a piece of software.

The Cons: The field is getting crowded; competition from big software companies with extremely deep pockets may mean a long, hard struggle, unless you target the markets that they've neglected.

Special Considerations: The appetite for new software is pretty enormous. As with other types of publishing, focusing on a particular niche increases your chances of success.

Profile
Alan Canton
PUB123
Adams-Blake Company
www.adams-blake.com
Fair Oaks, California

The best products sometimes come out of the frustration someone feels when trying to reinvent the wheel. In the case of publishing software, another bonus is that people have become dependent on computers because these RAM and ROM masters don't mind doing the drudgery, like people do.

Alan Canton developed a software program called PUB123 because, as a small book publisher, he became frustrated trying to tweak existing accounting software programs to accommodate the requirements of a publishing concern, such as differences in royalty rates paid to authors and books that retailers return for credit.

Of course, if you set out to reinvent the wheel, it helps if you've taken a course or two in wheel-making already. Canton was a publisher second and a programmer first, so he was already familiar with writing computer code and dealing with the inevitable bugs that arise. Canton originally wrote PUB123 for his own use, without a thought of marketing it to other publishers, but one thing led to another, and soon he was in the software-publishing business as well.

"Others publishers would ask us what we used, and we'd send them a copy of the program," says Canton. "Even though it was hardly full-featured, it was simple and did all the basics a small publisher needed. People loved it and told us we should package it and sell it, and I didn't believe it, but after the twentieth person told me this, I thought that maybe I had something here." He took three months off from his regular publishing duties and started from scratch, writing a new, reliable program with a friendly interface, and the rest is history, as he puts it.

One way Canton was ahead of corporate software manufacturers was that he made a conscious effort to distribute the program exclusively over the Internet, instead of selling it in stores or through the mail. As a result, Adams-Blake receives lots of feedback, negative and positive, about the program, such as features his customers want to see in future versions of the program. "It's easy for us to fix bugs and to alert our user base to new releases and features," he says.

Canton markets PUB123 through e-mail, exhibiting at publishing trade shows, and by advertising in industry magazines, but he says that word of mouth serves him best. He decided to keep the price low—$99 as opposed to the four-figure price tags of other publishing-specific accounting software—in order to start a buzz about the program.

Canton has a unique perspective on the similarities and the differences of book and software publishing. For one, he believes it's easier to get people interested in software than in books. "The world is awash with books," he says, "Software is different, and because software is interactive, people have different experiences with it, and they like to talk about those experiences. It also has a higher perceived value than a book."

Because of that interactivity, however, the publisher needs to invest more time and effort into keeping the dialogue going. "When you sell a book, that's the end of it," he says. "When you sell software, you are just beginning a relationship with the buyer, and you have to give good service, since that is one of the things that will sell the product. But this is why we kept the program easy to use—we didn't want our phone to endure a meltdown from everyone and their dog calling to ask questions."

After PUB123 had been on the market for a year, Canton was surprised to discover that many book publishers also had sideline businesses, like graphics, seminars, and consulting. As a result, they begin to ask him to incorporate nonpublishing features into the program, like file exporting and label making, which led him to create a new product called SOHO-123, for the small office/home office market.

Canton says that without special technological knowledge, you might as well forget publishing software. "Creating software for today's sophisticated machines is difficult," he says. "When all computers had were characters à la DOS, it was easy to program. But today's computer user is sophisticated and used to all the whiz-bang features they see in software that costs millions of dollars to produce. In order to produce visual software, you need a lot of very specialized, technical knowledge. If it were easy, there would be as many software packages as there are books."

His advice for aspiring software publishers is to test, test, and test again. "You need to test the market to see if there is a need for the product," he says. "You need to test the price point to see what people will pay, and you need to test the program so you don't get a bad rep for producing buggy software.

"The best niche is the one where a successful product already exists but costs an arm and a leg. If you can come up with a program that does 80 percent of what the leading product does and you can price it 90 percent lower, you have a great chance of being successful."

Zines

◆

Description of Business: A company that publishes a low-budget, quirky periodical called a *zine,* which serves more as a forum for the publisher/editor's opinions than as a vehicle for information and advice.

Ease of Startup: Easy. All you need is a typewriter or computer and access to a copy machine

Range of Initial Investment: $100 and up.

Time Commitment: Part-time

Success Potential: Difficult, if you want to make any money. Easy, if all you want to do is circulate your writing.

How to Market the Business: Over the Internet, through other zines, and by passing them out to friends, family, co-workers, and total strangers.

The Pros: It's easy to start a zine, and if you've always been frustrated by receiving rejection slips from other publications, your troubles will be over.

The Cons: Don't expect to make any money publishing a zine. You'll be lucky to break even.

Special Considerations: Publishing a zine can be great for the ego and create a way for you to be in touch with lots of other people who share your ideas. But be prepared to view your zine as more of a social outlet than a profit-maker.

Profile
Kathy Biehl
Ladies' Fetish & Taboo Society
Compendium of Urban Anthropology
Houston, Texas

Like many publishers, Kathy Biehl started a zine, called *Ladies' Fetish & Taboo Society Compendium of Urban Anthropology*, because she had some ideas that she wanted to share with her friends as well as with other people. Of course, the version of the zine that she publishes today doesn't much resemble her early efforts.

"It all started in 1988 as a series of photocopied pages of bizarre things that had caught my eye in law journals and in newspapers," Biehl says. She found these items to be so weird that she just had to share them with her friends. At first, she just collected little tidbits of incredibly odd stuff, taped it to pieces of paper, brought it to Kinko's, and ran off copies to send to friends. The first couple of years, Biehl sent these copies out whenever her drawer full of odd tidbits began to overflow, which happened about once a year.

She says that she started publishing the zine to prove to people that this odd-ball stuff really happens and adds that the zine has contained several running themes over the years, such as frustration with bureaucracy and gender confusion. When

the publication started to circulate, she received letters from people all over the world. "Complete strangers would write to me, pouring their guts out, telling me about the strange things that had happened to them," she says. "As a result of publishing the zine, I have developed very unusual friendships, and all kinds of people send me strange stories about things they've overheard at the grocery store, or unbelievable things that have happened to them at the bureaucracies where they work." In this way, a lot of Biehl's research for the zine is done for her, though she still contributes a lot of her own experiences to the publication.

Each issue of *Ladies' Fetish & Taboo Society Compendium of Urban Anthropology* is 16 pages, unless Biehl gets way behind schedule. Then she publishes a double issue of 24 pages. She tries to publish a new issue four times a year, but admits that the official publication schedule is "whenever," and actually states this on her masthead. Such is the flexibility of publishing a zine; you couldn't get away with this if you were publishing a magazine or newsletter, but in the world of zine publishing, it's expected and almost encouraged.

A subscription to *Ladies' Fetish & Taboo Society Compendium of Urban Anthropology* costs $10 for four issues ($14 for subscribers who live outside the United States). Biehl doesn't accept paid advertising, but she will barter advertising for other zines and products that strike her fancy. With no advertising revenue, she must pay her expenses solely from subscriptions; she breaks even with 200 subscribers. Like virtually every zine publisher, Biehl doesn't do it for the money. "I do it as an alternative to therapy," she admits, and adds that she's worked as a freelance writer since 1982. Publishing a zine is the only way to say things that no one else would dare to print. When she started the zine, it cost her only a few dollars; now she spends around $300 on photocopying and another $100 for postage.

Indeed, *Ladies' Fetish & Taboo Society Compendium of Urban Anthropology* is eclectic, cheeky, and well written, but I see where it would go over the heads of many people. Biehl says that a lot of people have written to her to say how much they *hate* her zine. "It's very quirky," she says. "You have to read the print zine fairly closely, but by the end of an issue it all starts to make sense." She describes her audience as ranging in age from their mid-twenties to mid-forties, and extremely well read. Though they're mostly college educated, they tend to be overeducated and underemployed. "I've never run a survey of my readers, but there seem to be certain themes that they have in common, which include a good knowledge of classical music and a familiarity with gay and alternative lifestyles, though it is not a gay publication," says Biehl.

Her renewal rate on the zine hovers around 65 percent, so to keep the zine going, she must constantly scout for new readers. She trades subscriptions with other zine publishers, expecting that some of the other zines will review *Ladies' Fetish & Taboo Society Compendium of Urban Anthropology* and that their readers will subscribe. She also sends a subscription to a publication called Factsheet Five, which is considered the mother of all zines. "It's a zine that exists to review zines and other small publications with thumbnail listings of anything they think has merit," she explains. "It's published twice a year, and, in fact, I get most of my requests for sample issues through Factsheet Five."

She also promotes her zine by reprinting excerpts from the publication on her Web site, but she is opposed to placing each complete issue there because it's very easy for anybody to steal her work. She says that one of the best things she's ever written, an essay called "101 Ways to Sabotage Your Date," had been downloaded and sent to a humor Usenet group. The members of that group then circulated the essay over the Internet, which can reach tens of thousands of people in a matter of hours. Biehl was unaware that her work was being circulated until a subscriber stumbled on a few cases where people had downloaded her essay and passed it off as their own. As a result, she is very selective about what she will place on the Web.

Another way that she promotes her zine is through an electronic newsletter called *Demitasse*, which contains articles and teasers that Biehl doesn't plan to publish in the zine. "It's a blatant pitch for people to subscribe," she admits. She also spends lots of time surfing the Internet. Anytime that she finds a Web page that is particularly well written and might attract the type of people who would appreciate her zine, and it has a site that reviews other publications, she'll send a note to the Webmaster asking him or her to visit her page and consider including it on the review site.

Besides freelance writing, Biehl also works as a self-employed attorney, which is why she considers her publication schedule to be "whenever." Because she views her zine as a way to get her thoughts out into the world, and not as a way to make money, she isn't pressured by the bottom line like other publishers.

Often it seems that zine publishers exist solely to communicate with other zine publishers. "In the underground publishing world, there is a vast network of people who are involved in producing zines to varying degrees, and a lot of us end up in communication with each other through the mail and e-mail," says Biehl. "We frequently trade things back and forth, and give each other ideas and sometimes leads, though this field of publishing doesn't seem to have the element of cutthroatness to it that other forms do."

In the past, Biehl's zine has been sold on a wholesale level through a distributor and has appeared on bookstore and magazine shelves, but she admits that it doesn't have a tremendous amount of shelf appeal. "It does contain some graphics," she says, "but it doesn't have a glossy cover and it's not splashy at all." In fact, her zine is very text heavy, which, in a sense, is to be expected because she's deliberately parodying academic style.

Biehl intends to keep her quirky publication in the form of a zine. "I wouldn't want to do it as a magazine because it would cost more and I don't have the time," she says. "With this kind of format you can get away with an awful lot. The content to me is more important than the way that I present it, though I do want it to look tidy. Some zine publishers will paste stuff together, reproduce images, make collages, and play with their graphics programs, but I don't have the time to spare."

Biehl comments on two disadvantages to publishing a zine: "First, you are not going to make any money at it and you're lucky if you break even," she says. "Second, by publishing a zine, you open yourself up to some pretty nasty criticism. It's astonishing, the zine world is like any social group, and there are cliques and people who take it upon themselves to pass judgment on other people. I have received some phenomenally vicious reviews and I never did anything to these people, and you can get your ego bent out of shape if you take it seriously."

But she'll continue to publish, both for the joy of getting her words out into the world and for the feedback and encouragement that she receives from kindred spirits who are far, far away. "It makes you feel a lot less alone," she says.

Ezines and Webzines

✦

Description of Business: A company that produces a regular newsletter or magazine and publishes it electronically, on a Web site or through e-mail.

Ease of Startup: Easy. If you have a focused idea, an audience, a computer, and appropriate software, you can start.

Range of Initial Investment: $2,000 for computer and software.

Time Commitment: Part- or full-time.

Success Potential: Moderate. Some ezines rely on advertising revenues while others serve as an infomercial for their other products and services. Content is king, particularly with Web-based ezines, and generating sufficient original content to keep visitors coming back can be expensive.

How to Market the Business: Through e-mail signatures, URLs on your business cards, listings in all of your printed correspondence, and by including it everywhere you would otherwise list your phone number.

The Pros: It's ridiculously easy to get an ezine and Webzine up and running these days; knowledge of html and computer code is unnecessary.

The Cons: You shouldn't expect to derive your primary income from a Webzine or ezine; instead view it as a supplement to other segments of your publishing empire.

Special Considerations: Publishing a Webzine or ezine that focuses on a very specific audience that is not being effectively served can quickly build you a sizable and loyal audience.

Profile
Pamela Wilfinger
Inscriptions, a weekly ezine for
professional writers
Florida

The best kind of business to start—publishing or other—usually revolves around a passion. Being an entrepreneur automatically translates into passion for business, a hobby, or simply a desire to make things right.

Pamela Wilfinger was destined to write about writing because, she says, from a very early age writing was indeed a passion. She became a reporter for her school newspaper in her junior year of high school. During her senior year, she was appointed editor-in-chief, a responsibility she juggled while holding down a part-time position at a local community weekly newspaper.

"I love everything about writing," Wilfinger says, "from struggling for the right word to dealing with rejection." Plus, she adds, fewer audiences are more passionate about their work than writers.

In 1998, she was working full-time as the editor for an ezine called *Eye on the Web* and she loved her job. One day, her boss told her the ezine was being terminated because the investors had backed out. Not only was she out of a job, but she was put in the unenviable position of firing all 300 of her freelance writers.

Wilfinger was devastated; as a result of her efforts, the ezine had won more than 22 awards from Web recognition sites. She halfheartedly sent out resumes to other ezines and online publications, before it hit her that she was acting selfishly: "Not only had I lost my job," she said, "but so had 300 wonderful writers."

That's when the brainstorm for *Inscriptions* hit. The ezine would be a weekly publication sent via e-mail and posted on her Web page, filled with news about new publications and markets looking for freelance writers, contests, book reviews, and more. "As long as I was looking for new work, I felt I should share this information with my old writers," she reports.

She chose both e-mail and a Web page to deliver *Inscriptions* in order to reach the widest audience possible. "Everyone online has an e-mail address, but many people still don't have access to the Web," she says. Plus, many people who don't live in the United States must pay by the minute to gain access to the Web, so Wilfinger figured a text-only ezine would cut down on their costs.

Wilfinger loves the challenge of writing and editing, but like many writers she's not crazy about selling. *Inscriptions*, of course, is available free to anyone who subscribes, but it costs money and time to gather the articles, manage the mailing list, and produce and distribute the publication.

"The only way to create a successful ezine is to provide useful, informative, original content, and this costs money. Because we are not backed by investors, and our advertising dollars haven't even begun to match our costs, it's been difficult to find quality articles and reviews," she says. Like many ezines, Wilfinger cannot afford to pay for articles and reviews, but she has a stable of professionals who respect her efforts to dig up paying markets to list in the ezine, so they contribute articles or otherwise volunteer their time to work with the publication.

In the first year of publication, she's solicited five regular advertisers and participates in affiliate programs with Amazon, CyberPress, and other companies that pay referring companies like *Inscriptions* when a subscriber makes a purchase through the ezine.

Though Wilfinger has no plans to convert the ezine to a print version, she does strive to make *Inscriptions* the best source of information available online for freelance writers. She also plans to expand her Web site to include daily horoscopes and cartoons, best-selling book lists, and other writing-related content.

Wilfinger recommends that the first rule for any ezine publisher to follow is to think about your readers first and foremost. "They are a hungry audience," she says, "and it's up to you to provide great content, information that is useful to their lives." She admits that the best way to accomplish this is to hire professional writers and editors to work with you. After all, with amazing content, thousands of people, if not more, can benefit from reading your ezine.

PART THREE

The Business of Running Your Home-Based Publishing Business

Defining Your Home-Based Publishing Business

✦

ONCE YOU start to narrow down what kind of home-based publishing business you want to start, it's a good idea to have all of the broad strokes confirmed so you can start planning the details that you'll need to have in place before you can begin.

If you haven't yet narrowed down the type of publishing business you'd like to run, exactly what you want to do, or if you can't decide between several of the ideas you have for a business, it's a good idea to write out plans for each of them. Sometimes just seeing the specifics in black and white can help you make your final decision.

Keep in mind that some of your answers to these questions will become more refined and detailed as you continue to read this book.

Refining Your Idea

YOU MAY already have an idea for the type of publishing business you'd like to run. Great—the next thing you need to do is refine your idea, check out your competition, and put your own unique spin on the topic.

My point in taking you through this step-by-step process is to make sure that your home-based publishing business will serve a purpose while addressing the problems of a particular market that is relatively easy to reach. I feel that these are the first issues that any business owner should address before starting a new venture.

During the course of your research, if you discover that a competitor has already beaten you to your idea, just twist your idea some more: Either slant it toward another market, or specialize in a particular group of people or businesses. For instance, if someone is already publishing a newsletter that tells doctors how they can utilize the Internet and World Wide Web to market their businesses, you can go after lawyers, restauranteurs, or florists. Focusing on a particular group will make it easier to reach them than if you just say that you're going to publish a newsletter on how any business owner can market with the Internet.

To begin, get a notebook and sketch out the details of your home-based publishing business by asking yourself the following questions.

+ What kind of publishing business would you be happy with? Be as specific as possible.

+ Can you run it full-time or part-time while you keep your present job?

+ When do you want to start your business?

+ How much time do you need to plan your business?

+ How can your friends and family help you?

+ How much money do you need to start your business?

+ How do you think you're going to spend the majority of your time when you're working on your business?

Do Your Homework

OVERALL, NO matter what type of publishing business you decide you want to start, the amount of research you do before you open your doors is critical to the potential success of your business—in most cases.

In time, you may discover that once you've researched and planned what you're going to do, you'll see that you do indeed have the courage to go ahead with it, which is something that even entrepreneurs who have been in business for decades still experience. Many people check out absolutely everything, from the geographic location of their businesses to taking specialized classes in their field as well as lining up mentors they can turn to when they need some feedback. This last step also ensures that you'll have a ready network of supportive people set up before you ever make the change.

How Much Time Do You Need to Plan Your Home-Based Publishing Business?

SOME PEOPLE decide what kind of home-based publishing business they want to run, then jump right in that same day, week, or month. Most people need a little more time. Deciding how much time you're going to need to plan your business is not an exact science; it depends on you. Some people plan for three months when they could have benefited more from six months of planning, while others who took a year find that they could have started marketing their business and soliciting customers after only six months of planning.

The amount of time you need to plan your home-based publishing business primarily depends on you and your financial situation as well as the faith you have in your abilities. If you need to plan every little detail in order to feel confident enough to start a business, then you should take up to a year or more. If you feel that the longer you put it off, the more likely that running your own business will just remain a good idea and not reality, then by all means, do whatever is necessary to get your affairs in order, then plunge right in, perhaps only after a couple of months of planning.

What Will Your Home-Based Publishing Business Look Like?

IT'S DIFFICULT to know exactly what running your home-based publishing business will be like until you open your doors. But once you start planning, it's likely that you will have a clearer picture of what you're going to be doing. In your notebook, write down your answers to the following.

+ What expectations do you have about the business you've chosen?

+ Are you prepared to switch gears if your business starts to disappoint you? How do you think you'll do it?

+ What external motivations will you set up to keep you going?

+ Brainstorm: Write down a schedule of the perfect day running your business.

Quick, what are your impressions of entrepreneurial life? If you're like most people interested in starting a home-based publishing business, having control over your life, making some money, and pursuing your favorite activity are probably at the top of your list.

I'd bet that the main reason you want to start your own business is because your present life offers none of the above.

Obviously, you think that running your own business would eliminate some of the biggest pains in your life while creating several new ones that you've never had to deal with before.

Some people start their own home-based publishing businesses not because they have a burning desire to be an entrepreneur, but because they hate their current lives. These people tend not to last more than two years in their own businesses before they turn right around and get a full-time job working for somebody else again.

Getting Real

To PUT it bluntly, starting your own home-based publishing business is about changing your entire life. That's why it's important to get real about why you want to become an entrepreneur in the first place. The first step is to deal with the fact that you're leaving your seemingly secure, known life behind you. In my experience, the number one reason people don't start their own businesses when they really want to is because they think they won't be able to make any money at it. The number two reason is security: Even though you may hate your present life, it's all you know and it's familiar. Though you may have developed a mental image of entrepreneurial life from articles and TV shows that tout the advantages of the

lifestyle—usually without ever mentioning any of the disadvantages, I might add—you probably still are not clear on what it will be like for you. Will you be able to make it? Will you be able to pay the bills? Whatever's holding you back, it's likely that one or all of these concerns are major issues for you.

So before you begin to dream about the kind of business you'd like to run or what your daily life will be like, take some time to figure out *why* you want to change your life.

Everyone has their own reasons for wanting to run their own business. If you're not clear about these reasons before you start—and if you do it for what I think of as the wrong reasons—you may discover that once you become responsible for your own publishing business you won't want to put up with the tough stuff, since you had no idea what to expect.

Much as you want to view a move into entrepreneurial self-sufficiency as an instant metamorphosis, transforming your life into everything you've ever wanted, you have to realize that many of your old problems will still be around. I compare this outlook to that of a person who believes losing ten pounds will make his or her life perfect. "If I could only quit my job and start my own business, my life will magically change for the better." Though there are some pragmatic people who don't subscribe to this philosophy, I know that many people do. Therefore, the clearer your reasons for what you hope to accomplish by starting your own business, the more successful your transition into entrepreneurial life will be.

In your notebook, write the answers to the following questions, to help you to get clear about the *why* behind your decision to strike out on your own. Even though you may already have a good idea of why you want to start your own business, answering the following questions will help you to focus in on your true motivations. Answer the following questions honestly and go into as much detail as you need. Then keep your answers in mind as you continue to read.

+ Why do you want to start your own home-based publishing business? Give five reasons and rank them in order of importance.

+ What do you want to know how to do after you've been running your publishing business for a year? How do you propose to learn about it?

+ Describe your fantasy publishing business and everything about it.

+ What do you like about your current job?

+ What do you hate about your current job?

+ What do you want to learn in the process of starting your own business?

+ What could you do today to bring you one step closer to running your home-based publishing business?

+ What's your biggest excuse for *not* starting your business today?

Brainstorm: Quickly make a list of 50 things that you associate with being an entrepreneur. Think about how they'll fit into your life once you start your home-based publishing business. Write them down even if they make no sense. Then cross out the half that are less important. Take the remaining 25 and ponder their place in your life and whether they fall under the category of fantasy, reality, or a little of both.

Visualizing Your Home-Based Publishing Business

NOW IS the perfect time to fantasize about exactly how you visualize your home-based publishing business. You may want to answer these questions twice, once for how you view your business when you're first starting out, and again a year or more later, after you have gained some experience and perspective about what it's really like to run a business and have a clearer idea about your plans for the future. If you're starting your business with a partner, both of you should separately answer these questions and compare your answers. If any of your answers are radically different, you should address them now to avoid unnecessary expense and disagreements later.

+ What will you name your company?

+ What will be your primary product or service? What will be some secondary services?

+ Will you devote yourself to your business full- or part-time? If part-time, how long will you run it in this way?

+ What type of people will use what you have to sell?

+ Describe the overall tone of your business, lush and expensive or spartan?

+ How and where will you market your business?

+ What will make your business stand out?

+ Who are your competitors? How will your business be different?

Writing Your Business Plan

WHY SHOULD you have a business plan? By this time, you have some idea about what kind of home-based publishing business you want to run and when you will start. Even if your goals are not very specific at this point, you probably know that you would rather publish books than a magazine, for example.

Writing a business plan will help you to map out a specific blueprint to follow on your way to meeting your business goals. A business plan leaves no question about the smallest aspect of getting your business off the ground; in the confusion and excitement of being a new entrepreneur, after all, many things get overlooked. Getting it all down in writing will provide you with a detailed itinerary. Because you write the plan yourself, you'll be able to tailor it to your own needs and to tinker with it later, when unforeseen roadblocks begin to emerge.

With a business plan in hand, you'll be able to show the bank, your suppliers, and other potential business contacts exactly how you visualize your business, in language and figures they understand. But writing reveals a lot as it unfolds. Not only will your business plan provide you with a broad picture of your business, in addition to allowing you to get all of the little details down in writing, but you'll also think of other things as you think, write, and plan aspects of your prospective business that might not have come up otherwise.

Writing a business plan before you do anything else for your business will put you way ahead of your competition, since most businesses do not take the time to carefully plan out their strategies. I know—sometimes I haven't written a business or marketing plan before starting a business, and I paid for it down the road when I became unfocused about exactly what I wanted to accomplish. However, it's never too late to write a business plan.

A business plan is vital to the successful startup of a business, so you shouldn't tuck it away in a drawer and forget about it. It is meant to be used and referred to as you progress in your home-based publishing business. Periodically checking the progress you're making against the plan allows you to see where changes need to be made, as well as whether you're keeping up with, or even surpassing, your original goals.

As I've mentioned, one of the top reasons why businesses fail is due to a lack of planning. Writing a detailed business plan that is geared toward your ideal will let you see whether your goals fit your budget, whether you should wait until you've raised more money, or indeed, whether this is the right type of publishing business for you after all.

Anyone who reads your business plan will be able to get a clear picture of the type of business you want to run, as well as its projected financial health.

SAMPLE BUSINESS PLAN

A business plan can be only a few pages long or a massive 100-page document that maps out every single detail involved in running your home-based publishing business.

Though it takes more time, it's best to err on the side of quantity when writing a business plan. The more you know about your publishing business before your first customer walks through the door or calls on the phone, the better prepared you will be for surprises.

A business plan should have six sections: a cover sheet; a statement of purpose for the business; a table of contents; a description of the business, including what you provide, your target markets, your location, competition, and personnel you expect to hire; financial information such as income and cash flow projections, or, if you're buying a business from another owner, the financial history of the business; and supporting documents, such as your resume, your credit report, letters of reference, and any other items you believe will help. For an example of a business plan, see the Appendix A.

Starting a Home-Based Publishing Business from Scratch

IF YOU decide to start your business from scratch, you will need to do more work than if you buy an existing business. The advantage of starting your own business is that it costs less; it will also bear your personal stamp from the outset. Buying someone else's business means that you'll have to work within a successful format and style that may not fit your own. You'll have to tinker with the formula slowly—and even then, you may lose customers. You will also need to work hard on developing and building your reputation. There's also a lot more detail and legal work to do if you start from scratch.

The main disadvantage to starting a business from scratch is that you won't have income from the business until you start attracting customers, which usually takes longer than your initial estimates. In fact, while you do pay more at the outset for an existing business, the business can start producing revenue from the day you take over, since once you assume ownership, you also keep any new business and revenue that comes in after the transfer of ownership. You should weigh the pros and cons before you proceed with buying an existing business. I find that the vast majority of home-based publishing entrepreneurs start their own businesses from scratch because the type of product they want to produce doesn't exist.

If you buy an existing business, most of the business technicalities have already been set up for you, from registering your business name to handling insurance for your business, though you do have to change everything over into your name.

If you decide to purchase an existing business instead of starting your own, you

have a track record you can compare your own efforts to, though you still need to write a business and marketing plan.

An established publishing business comes with a built-in reputation and a well-developed list of customers loyal to the business. Sometimes buying an existing business actually costs less than starting from scratch, if you factor in the reputation of the business, the customer list, computer equipment, and other amenities that are included in the purchase price. If you figure that your labor is worth something, even though you probably won't be paying yourself a salary for quite some time, buying a business outright may turn out to be a veritable bargain.

I once sold a newsletter I had been publishing for a couple of years to the company that was handling my circulation duties. When the owner's lawyer sent me the first contract to arrange the sale, it included a clause that stated that after the sale transpired, I would be responsible for refunding the money to any customer who cancelled his or her subscription. My lawyer struck the clause from the contract, and the buyer accepted it without a whimper. It's a good thing we removed the clause, because after the buyer took it over, the new owner completely changed the direction of the business and ended up folding it after only two issues.

Your Home-Based Publishing Business and the Law

WITH ANY business, whether or not it involves publishing, there are certain legal requirements that you have to meet in order to do business. The first thing you need to do is register your business with your state government. There will be a fee for this, and the purpose is to make sure no other business is currently operating with your name. If there is, you will have to find another name for your business.

Registration also alerts the state to expect tax revenue from your business. If you don't file a return with your state tax authorities each year, they'll know where to find you.

When you register with the state, you should ask about other regulations you have to meet in order to operate as a home business. Most of the time, officials will refer you to your town, which is responsible for determining zoning and other business regulations, and issue any permits for renovations that you will need to do.

I will get into the nitty gritty of the various bureaucracies later in this chapter. The important thing at this point is to find out what departments the state, town, or county are each responsible for, the type of registration you will have to make with each, and to make sure you comply with all of them. If you neglect any one of the steps necessary to open and operate a business in your town, the government authorities have the power to shut down your business or do whatever is necessary in order to bring your business into compliance. The time to find all of this out is before you open your doors. So it pays to do your homework first.

You'll also need to determine the form of business you'll run: a sole proprietorship, partnership, or a corporation. Each has advantages and disadvantages, and home-based business owners have very specific reasons for picking one over the others.

SOLE PROPRIETORSHIP

A sole proprietorship is the form of business that most single-owner businesses pick. It's easy to start—all you have to do is register with the state and check that your local zoning laws allow a home office such as you have in mind. You don't need to worry about partnership contracts—you alone are responsible for the success or failure of your business, and any profits that your business earns are reported as income in your name.

However, because there are few restrictions on a sole proprietorship when you run into legal or financial trouble, it falls on your shoulders to deal with it. For many home-based publishing entrepreneurs, liability insurance that's tied in with your business or homeowners policy will often be enough to handle a "reasonable" lawsuit and settlement. The remote chances of being hit with a lawsuit and the relative ease of operating this form of business ownership make a sole proprietorship the preferred method of business organization for most home-based publishing entrepreneurs.

If your business should fail, you will be responsible for all outstanding debts incurred during the course of doing business. If you don't pay them, or declare bankruptcy, it will be reflected on your personal credit record.

PARTNERSHIP

A partnership is actually two sole proprietorships combined into one. This means that while the strengths are doubled, so are the inherent weaknesses.

The most common instance where an entrepreneur decides to create a partnership is when he or she chooses to enter the business with a friend or business partner. Married couples also sometimes decide to form a partnership when they start a business together. Though a partnership usually means that twice as much more energy and money is available than

in a sole proprietorship, if you're thinking about forming a partnership, you should consider it very carefully before you proceed. Partnerships work best when the partners have differing but complementary talents and each leaves the other partner alone to do what he or she does best. For instance, one partner may have a strong background in marketing and day-to-day business operations, while the other loves researching different markets and reporting the results, which the other can use to define the market. As long as each trusts the other to concentrate on his or her own department and to interfere only when problems arise, the partnership will probably do well.

Partnerships usually run into trouble when the partners have similar skills and/or different ideas about the right way to run a business. For example, when both partners want to concentrate on sales but not on the behind-the-scenes tasks like bookkeeping and managing the office, there are going to be problems right from the start.

As with a sole proprietorship, if somebody decides to sue the business, usually for libel or remarks that the subject perceives as inflammatory, both partners are personally liable. And if the business fails, leaving outstanding debts, you are both responsible. You should also be aware that if one partner disappears after a business fails, the other must pay all debts. Be aware of this, because this does happen from time to time.

CORPORATION

A corporation is best defined as a legal entity that is separate and distinct from its owners. It's more difficult, expensive, and time-consuming to form and then operate your business as a corporation, but doing so also absolves your formal personal responsibility in case business sours or a customer decides to sue.

Another advantage that corporations have over partnerships and sole proprietorships is that a corporation can raise money by selling shares in the business; the only recourse the other two have is to borrow money from a bank or from friends.

But a corporation is by nature more unwieldy because of its responsibility to its shareholders, who are really part owners. The IRS taxes corporations on a different scale from sole proprietorships and partnerships, and there are more rules and regulations a corporation must follow on both the state and federal level. There are also certain restrictions on the types of operations a corporation can run—some expansion and growth issues, for example, require the approval of stockholders before a project can proceed.

Some publishing entrepreneurs automatically opt for incorporation to protect their personal assets in the case of a lawsuit, and this is prudent. However, the type of business that will benefit most from incorporation is when there are more than two owners controlling the future of the business. With multiple partners deciding the fate of the business, issues of ownership and decision-making necessarily become more complex, so it becomes easier to rely on a board of directors and group of stockholders, especially since they've invested their money and trust in the business.

Do You Need An Attorney?

WHETHER OR not you choose to use the services of an attorney to help you set up your home-based publishing business depends on how you view the legal profession as well as how detail-oriented you are. Some home-based publishing entrepreneurs swear by their lawyers and consult with them about every decision that needs to be made. Others swear *at* them and will never use an attorney for anything in their business or personal lives.

The happy medium is somewhere in between. If you're planning to incorporate your business, you'll probably need to use a lawyer, although more people are learning how to incorporate themselves. I feel that the vast majority use a lawyer to help facilitate the process and because their minds are elsewhere.

If, however, you're buying an established publishing business, you will undoubtedly have to hire an attorney to negotiate the terms of the contract. Aside from this, you will probably be able to do most of the tasks involved in starting your business without a lawyer.

Do You Need An Accountant?

I F Y O U ' R E unsure about the type of business organization that suits you best—sole proprietorship, partnership, or corporation—it's a good idea to consult an accountant to help you decide. An accountant can analyze your current financial situation to help you determine what you want to gain from your business in terms of revenue—equity or income— and advise you about how to best achieve your goals.

An accountant can also analyze the books and financial records of a publishing business that you're thinking about buying. It's a good idea to find an accountant who has some experience keeping the books for small companies in your field; you may want to ask other small business owners in your area for the names of some accountants they'd recommend to you. Then call and interview them before you settle on one.

An accountant can also help you set up a realistic budget and a schedule of projected revenues. If this is the first time you've run a business of your own, an accountant can also help you become familiar with different accounting methods and the tax rates based on projected revenue and the tax codes of your state. He or she can also recommend methods of bookkeeping that will make the job that much easier when tax season rolls around.

Licenses and Permits

B E F O R E Y O U open for business, you must check with the local, county, and state business authorities to find out what kinds of licenses and permits you'll need to meet in order to be licensed, if any.

I will, however, describe the purpose of the licenses and permits you will be required to get. Bear in mind, however, the stringency of these requirements varies. States and regions with more highly regulated governments tend to be pickier about what you can and cannot do with your home-based publishing business, and the fees they charge you for the privilege of making enough money to pay taxes.

Even though you may resent all the legalese and paperwork, it's important to meet all of the requirements. No one says you can't complain every step of the way, however.

You'll need a sales tax certificate from the state to collect tax on any in-state mail-order purchases your customers make from you.

Even if your home and facilities successfully meet all of the regulations, if your home is not in an area that is zoned for business, you may be out of luck and will need to run your business from an office in an area that's especially zoned for commercial use. Your town government determines zoning and is responsible for making exceptions for small businesses located outside of commercial zones. Though your business will provide a tax base for your town and help bring more money to local businesses that you frequent, because you will have a commercial enterprise operating in a residential area, you will probably have to apply for a zoning variance.

Some towns allow you to operate your business at home as long as you don't hang out a sign. You may also have to expand your driveway and parking area to accommodate an increased number of cars.

More laws governing small businesses in your area undoubtedly exist. That's why it's important to check all of the requirements before you do anything.

Hiring Employees

SOME HOME-BASED publishing entrepreneurs prefer to keep their operations as small, one-person businesses, specifically so they'll be able to handle all the jobs themselves without having to hire outside help. Hiring and managing employees adds a whole new dimension to your business and has both its good and bad points. For one, it means more paperwork because you'll have to pay state, federal, and perhaps local payroll taxes in addition to Social Security, worker's compensation, and insurance, if you decide to offer it. On the other hand, having someone around to help out with the grunt work means you'll have more time to focus on running and building your business, like marketing and exploring new services to provide to your growing customer base.

Unfortunately, a common complaint of business owners everywhere today is that it's hard to find good help; after all, no paid employee is going to regard your business and customers in the same light that you do. So you'll probably have to lower your standards of quality and attention and plan to spend some time making up for the lack.

With the rise in sexual harassment suits, many small business owners have been further discouraged from hiring help, even though they may want to.

Many entrepreneurs advise that if you find an employee who is the exception to the rule, hold onto him or her as tightly as you can by increasing pay, offering bonuses, and showing your appreciation with added responsibilities and an occasional day off with pay.

When hiring employees, there are certain things you have to do. If you're hiring a person to work for you regularly, answering the phone, running errands, and dealing with customers, he or she will be considered to be your employee and you will have to deduct taxes from his or her paycheck, which you will have to file with the government either quarterly or once a year, depending on your tax setup.

Some businesses get around the process of withholding and payroll taxes by preferring to hire an employee as an independent contractor. This way, the contractor files a self-employment tax, which saves you a lot of paperwork. This works for such seasonal and periodic workers such as gardeners and musicians, but it will send up red flags with the IRS if you try to hire a part-time office assistant in this way. If you do hire an independent contractor, and pay him or her more than $600 over the course of a year, you must file a 1099 form, which reports their income.

No matter how you decide to hire an employee, make sure that you always communicate clearly and directly and immediately when there's a problem or complaint and let them know when you think they did a job well done.

Zoning Regulations for Home Businesses

ONE OF the things you must consider when running your publishing business from your home is the zoning ordinances in your town. Zoning ordinances may not name which types of businesses can and cannot be run from a private home. Many zoning ordinances were enacted decades ago, when the majority of people working from home were in service businesses, which provided a steady stream of traffic into their neighborhood each business day. If you are planning to work quietly from home, you are unlikely to run into objections. Nonetheless, it is a good idea to check with your town or city clerk if you are setting up a home office.

Tax Regulations for Home-Based Publishing Businesses

BACK IN the 1970s home office tax deductions were plentiful. Working from home was usually done in a corner of the sewing room or on part of the dining room table and most was work that was taken home from the office. Either an employee had to bone up and polish an important presentation for the next day or he or she had to meet a deadline.

That corner of the sewing room and portion of the dining room table was typically written off as a business expense. Nowadays if you were to do that, you might as well draw little red flags all over your tax return, because the IRS is extremely sensitized to examine home offices, whether you run your business at home full-time or not.

You can deduct for a home office if it meets one of three important criteria set down by the IRS:

+ Your home office is a place where clients, customers, and colleagues meet on a regular basis.

+ You use your home office only to conduct business, which means you shouldn't be using it as a kids' playroom when you're not there, or a laundry room. Specifically, the IRS asks if the home office is the principal place of business, which means that if you're spending less than half your working hours there, you probably can't take the deductions.

+ If your home office is located in a separate building, even if you work fewer than three days at home, it's likely that all costs you incur in maintaining that separate building are deductible, including the equipment you use while there.

Of course, there are instances that may diverge from these three criteria. If you're in doubt, you should contact either your accountant or the IRS directly. If you'd like more information, contact the IRS to get a free copy of IRS Publication Number 587: *Business Use of Your Home.*

If you choose to take the deduction, you must fill out a separate form to attach to your return called Form 8829. In essence, since auditors are tougher on people who maintain home offices for any purpose, the mere fact that you're filing the form will raise a red flag. This explains why so many people don't bother to take the deduction at all, even if they qualify.

Because people who work at home in their own small businesses easily pass the test of deducting the cost of the office space, usually the IRS waves them on by. The sticky part comes if you're still working for someone else and receiving a regular salary, since some people who run part-time businesses in addition to working full-time for an outside employer consistently show a loss from the business. Your return will come under more scrutiny than if you just take the standard deduction from a full-time job, because you'll have to verify your write-offs with figures and logs that showed you actively pursued new customers for your sideline business.

Of course, the best thing to do is to confer with your accountant or other tax professional before you do anything. Examine all the pros and cons before you decide to deduct an expense. And remember, if one area of your tax return catches the eye of an auditor, the rest of your return won't escape notice, either.

The Tools You'll Use

◆

EVERY HOME-BASED publishing business has its own set of tools that are unique to that field. But even businesses that are opposites in every regard have certain tools in common, among them bookkeeping methods, standardized marketing tools like letterhead stationery, and the criteria they use when hiring employees.

Think of the points covered in this chapter as a foreign language, a way to talk about your business so that other business owners will know exactly what you're talking about. Once you master Business Talk 101, who knows what you'll be capable of accomplishing in your business!

Keeping the Books

EVEN IF you hated math in high school, keeping good financial records of every transaction that occurs in your home-based publishing business—whether it's checks you receive or a cash receipt for a highway toll paid while you were on the road for business—is a basic necessity. After all, every entrepreneur wants to know how much money the business is generating before and after expenses, to see what all of your hard work is worth.

The good news is that with an abundance of inexpensive, comprehensive accounting software, the accounting tasks for a home-based publishing business are easier and take less time than ever before, so you can see exactly how much you spent on office supplies during the third week in August, for instance. If you compare your income and expenses against the same week a month or a year ago, or against the figures in your business plan, you'll be able to catch slowdowns and remedy them while they're still small and before they get out of hand.

Here's a list of some of the information you'll want your bookkeeping system to supply you with on a daily or weekly basis, depending on how detailed you want to get:

✦ Available cash on hand

✦ Balances of any business-related bank accounts

✦ Total of sales and/or cash receipts

✦ Total of expenses (payroll, bills, petty cash, etc.)

✦ Total in accounts receivable with details on the balance and age of any past 30 days

✦ All of the above figures for the previous month's tallies

✦ Anything else critical to keeping tabs on your business

Another benefit of keeping good records and making the time to enter income and expenses into your electronic ledger once a week is that doing your taxes will be easier. If you file paper copies, to correspond with your computer files, in the unlikely case of a tax audit not only will you save a lot of money on accountant bills, but you'll be able to show receipts that back up a specific deduction in response to an auditor's questions.

There are two different kinds of accounting systems you can use to track expenses and revenue for your home-based publishing business: cash accounting and accrual accounting. Cash accounting is the simplest form: Income is recorded in your bookkeeping system the month when it is received and paid expenses and bills are recorded when the check is written and sent, even if the expense may have been incurred in a different month.

Accrual accounting is slightly more complicated but provides a more accurate picture of the financial health of a home-based publishing business. Basically, income and expenses are recorded in the month they were initially incurred and not necessarily in the month they were received or paid out. This form of accounting is more detailed because the bookkeeper must pay attention to end-of-month peculiarities, as well as when your bank normally credits your account with checks and credit card charges.

Most new home-based publishing entrepreneurs opt for the cash accounting method, because the accrual accounting method usually provides more details and requires more time than most people need. It's your call; your accountant will be able to help you with your decision.

Insurance

RUNNING ANY business is risky business. Making sure that your home-based publishing business is properly insured against every possible problem that may arise could fill a book—and it has. Some home-based publishing entrepreneurs decide to take risks as a matter of course, but when it comes to insurance some go whole hog and insure their business, facilities, employees, and even themselves against every possible hazard; others treat the topic of insurance lightly and insure for only the most catastrophic hazards.

You probably fall somewhere in the middle. An insurance agent may say that having no insurance is the most expensive option of all, but this means little to a new entrepreneur with big dreams and a small budget. When the most likely kinds of risks involve incidents where the total cost is less than the deductible, being fully covered turns out to be more folly than anything else.

With this said, here are the kinds of general business insurance entrepreneurial experts recommend for home-based publishing entrepreneurs.

LIABILITY INSURANCE

Liability insurance will cover you if a client or customer or even bystander or illegal trespasser is injured on your business premises. The premium depends on the square footage of your business space as well as the frequency with which clients and suppliers have to come to your place of business. With a home-based publishing business, standard homeowners insurance covers liability, although you will have to notify your insurer that you are operating a business on the premises.

AUTOMOBILE INSURANCE

Two types of auto insurance are necessary if employees drive a vehicle in the course of working for your business: auto liability insurance on all business vehicles and non-owned auto liability insurance, which covers an employee who needs to drive his or her own car or a vehicle not owned by you or the business. You'll need to get additional coverage for the tools and goods that are transported in a business vehicle; in case of theft or damage, standard business policy won't cover it.

FIRE INSURANCE

Fire insurance covers any fire damage to equipment, inventory, and the physical building if you are the owner; if you rent, it may be a good idea to add fire legal liability insurance to your policy, which would cover any fire damage to your part of your landlord's building. When getting fire insurance, make sure you choose replacement-value coverage. Your own inexpensive form of fire insurance is to regularly back up all computerized business files and data, and keep the extra files in another location. Insurance companies never reimburse for the actual value of lost data when it comes to your time or the intrinsic value of the stored information.

WORKERS' COMPENSATION INSURANCE

In most states and in most industries, if you have employees, you need workers' compensation insurance, which provides death and disability benefits to employees and/or employees' survivors. If your state doesn't require workers' compensation insurance and if one of your employees is injured, your business is still liable. Many state governments offer employers workers' compensation insurance through a state plan, which tends to be less expensive than comparable plans offered through insurance companies and agencies.

Other kinds of insurance you may choose for your home-based publishing business and your employees follow. Depending on your state, some govern-

ments require that businesses provide them for all workers.

+ Health and/or hospitalization insurance
+ Life insurance
+ Disability insurance
+ Credit insurance
+ Unemployment insurance
+ Environmental impact insurance
+ Bonds and surety insurance
+ Internal theft insurance

Taxes

TAXES ARE where the business structure you choose matters most: It determines when, where, and how much Uncle Sam and the other government branches extract from your business. Because each state has its own idiosyncrasies when it comes to calculating and then collecting tax, this section deals strictly with the federal tax system because it is the same for everyone, no matter which state you live in. The good news is that every penny you spend in the course of doing business can be deducted from your overall business revenue, which then reduces the amount of tax you pay to the federal government. That means that every item you list in your monthly budget (Chapter 15) will contribute toward whittling down the final line on your federal tax return. A caveat: In most cases, equipment, capital improvements, and business vehicles are not deductible all at once, but either partially or in stages. So before you purchase a brand-new vehicle for your business, check to see when you'll be able to deduct it, if at all.

Because you are a business owner, you have a dual role when it comes to taxes. On the one hand, you serve as a tax collector, taking payroll deductions for federal income tax, Social Security tax, and other taxes from your employees, and sales tax from your customers, and then pay them to the correct governmental department. On the other hand, you are responsible for paying taxes on the revenue the business creates and that are dependent on your business structure. These may include federal income tax, state income tax, and property tax.

If you are a sole proprietor, you calculate the personal tax you owe with Schedule C and include it on Form 1040, which you file once a year. A sole proprietor is also required to pay an estimated tax—calculated from the previous year's total paid income tax—each quarter.

A partnership files a report of annual revenue and expenses on Form 1065, U.S. Partnership Return of Income, but no tax is due with this form. Instead, each partner divides the profits or losses as specified in a partnership agreement and adds this information to Schedule E, Supplemental Income and Loss, which they file with their individual 1040 forms.

Both kinds of corporations file tax forms once a year. For most, the forms must be received by the Internal Revenue Service by March 15. A regular C corporation reports revenue and expenses with Form 1120, or the short Form 1120A. A subchapter S corporation files Form 1120S but is not responsible for taxes on profits and doesn't receive a credit in the case of a loss. Instead, an S corporation splits the profits among each of its shareholders who then receive a Schedule K-1, which lists their share of the income. The shareholders report this information on their individual 1040 form, along with Schedule E.

Business tax law can be complicated, even for a sole proprietorship, but the simplest piece of information is this: Tax code is always changing, and just because you were able to claim one type of expense as a deduction last year does not mean you will be able to claim it next year.

Working With Suppliers and Vendors

LARGE, ESTABLISHED companies have departments whose only responsibility is to buy for the company, including supplies for the office, vehicles for employees, phone service, and travel. Their titles usually are buyer or procurement manager. They also keep track of when the supplies arrive and know where they are stored.

What a luxury. Not only will you wish you had someone to do all this for you, but you'll probably wish you had the same budget.

Needless to say, you'll have to do all the work yourself. Even if you run a business based on the contents of your brain, you'll still need materials and supplies to help disseminate the information locked within to make it useful to clients.

So how do you locate the suppliers and vendors who will provide you with everything you need in order to run your business? The best sources for materials are the companies and businesses that you're already familiar with: the warehouse office supply stores, the online office supply catalogs, the cleaning supplies under the kitchen sink or at the local discount store. If you need items that are more business-related than you've required in the past, the *Yellow Pages* are a great resource to find vendors in your region, as well as give you ideas for other types of products and services that will help you grow your business.

The advantage of working with these vendors is that you can pick up the materials yourself whenever you need them, and there's usually no minimum order.

The downside is the cost; because you're not buying 25 boxes of copy paper at one time, you're probably paying more than you would if you were to buy them from a wholesaler or distributor. Plus, you either have to pay for the supplies when you pick them up or put the expense on your credit card, where you'll then have to pay interest on the purchase. If you deal with wholesalers and distributors, you'll probably be billed on a net 30 basis and still get a discount, which when you add it up from all your suppliers, adds up to a significant help to your cash flow every month. But you may not need 25 boxes of copy paper or be crazy about the idea of tying up so much capital in supplies. You probably also lack the storage space. In the beginning, the question you'll face is quantity versus price, and since you probably don't want to tie up a lot of money in supplies, you should pay the extra cost so you'll have the use of your money.

Another good source of supplies when you're first starting out—usually at a discount regardless of the quantity you need—is from the vendors listed by the local or national trade organization for your industry. For instance, when you join the trade association in your field, you'll probably get a membership card and a subscription to the monthly trade publication, but you'll likely also receive with it a list of approved vendors, companies that have agreed to provide their service or product to members at a discount, because it's a market they may not have tapped otherwise. When you place an order, you'll have to give your membership number. You get the lower quantity you need at a price that's more affordable than you'd be able to get on your own or at one of the superstores.

If you're not sure what supplies you will need to successfully operate your business, take a look at the advertisements in your trade association's monthly publication. Take note of the advertisers you think you may need to call on in the future, or even call them up now to get a copy of their catalog and price list. Should there be a product or service you know you need but you can't locate a company to provide it, call up your trade organization and ask the membership services director for leads.

Later, as your home-based publishing business grows, you'll start to deal with wholesalers, distributors, and sales reps who can work with you, offer free shipping and delivery, and set up an account for your business at reasonable terms. But as with everything, there are clear exceptions; in fact, you may discover that, all things considered, you still get the best price at the same old haunts you frequented before you became a home-based publishing entrepreneur. No matter what, once you set your priorities as to cost or convenience, there are plenty of vendors and suppliers around who will be more than happy to help your business grow.

Hiring Employees/Using Independent Contractors

HIRING EMPLOYEES—or deciding whether to take one on in the first place—can be one of the most difficult decisions a home-based publishing entrepreneur can make.

Not only can labor and all of the associated costs like insurance, additional equipment and supplies, and employer-paid taxes turn the employment section of your budget into your single largest expenditure, but you are now responsible for another person's livelihood. If your business should suffer a setback, even temporary, the fact that the costs associated with employees are the biggest line item for many home-based publishing businesses means that you may have to cut back. In good economic times and bad, letting an employee go is easily the most unpleasant part of being the boss. A close second is the inordinate amount of paperwork required by federal, state, and local governments for taxes, insurance, and other employee expenditures.

With that said, having employees can not only help you accomplish more work, therefore helping you grow more quickly, but having another person nearby who is familiar with the business and who possesses a completely fresh pair of eyes can help propel your business into the steady growth you need.

Before you write a help wanted ad or start asking around, make a list of the tasks you'd like your employee to handle. Does he or she need special skills? Do you need him to be in the office on a full- or part-time basis? Is there special equipment he or she will need? Be reasonable about the amount of work you would need an employee to handle.

Next, you'll have to decide what kind of salary or hourly wage to offer. Check the help wanted ads in the local paper to see what other companies are offering their employees. Granted, businesses that are just starting out frequently cannot afford the salaries and benefits of a larger, more established company, so if you can find some way to compensate for lower pay, do so. Some new entrepreneurs let their employees work at their homes part of the time, or let them choose their own hours. Many people who have to juggle family and work responsibilities would gladly take less money in order to have more flexibility in their lives.

To find employees, your opportunities are limitless. Of course, many companies advertise in the local newspaper, but some studies have suggested that newspaper ads actually bring in the smallest number of qualified applicants.

You can ask your state's department of employment to post your open position on their online bulletin board. They also have applications from qualified people on file, so they may already have a good

match when you call. Local college and school job banks have students who are willing to work part- or full-time in the summer or on graduation, and the good thing about hiring a student is that in essence you have a blank slate.

Private employment agencies are also good sources of qualified candidates, but they tend to charge a hefty fee—usually from 10 to 25 percent of an entry-level employee's first-year salary.

The Internet has proven to be a great source of technology-savvy, enthusiastic people all over the world. Not only can you place a help wanted ad on one of the Web sites that cater to job seekers and companies with jobs to fill, but newsgroups, mailing lists, and even personal Web sites can serve as forums for a job that needs to be filled. If you have a Web site devoted to your business, you can add a page that lists any open positions as well as the type of applicant you're looking for.

Hands down the best source of employees are the people you already know, whether they're colleagues, co-workers from a previous job, or even friends and family. Ask them if they know of anyone who fits the description, and ask them to put the word out among their circle of friends, acquaintances, and colleagues.

Whether the job market is tighter than a drum or people are lining up for jobs, your goal in searching for an employee shouldn't waver: You want the best-qualified candidates to consider for the position, whose aim is to help your business grow. Don't settle for a person who has less than you're looking for. If a qualified candidate isn't quite what you had in mind but is enthusiastic and seems like a quick learner, you can temporarily adjust your requirements: Slightly reduce the pay, hire on a probationary status, and challenge the employee in as many ways that you can to discover whether this is the right person for the job. A candidate may be so strong in one area that you may be willing to forego a lack in another area. Just as employees cherish flexibility in a job, employers should acquire a flexible attitude when it comes to their employees.

If you can't find exactly the kind of employee you want, you may decide to farm the work out. The advantage to using independent contractors is that in times of tight employment, you don't need to look far for help. The biggest plus, however, is that the two of you agree on a fee for the project, the contractor performs the work, you pay him or her, and that is the end of your commitment to that person, unless you provide more work. This means that you are not responsible for calculating tax and insurance deductions from a paycheck, or for sending them to the appropriate governmental agencies. An independent contractor is responsible for figuring and then paying his or her own taxes, not you. This can save you a mountain of paperwork and a lot of time. You'll probably pay a little more to an independent contractor on a per-hour or per-project basis, but you'll save that and more in time you'll spend on paperwork than if the contractor was your employee.

If you pay an independent contractor more than $600 over the course of a year, you'll have to prepare a 1099 tax form, on which you detail the exact amount of money paid out, along with the contractor's name, address, and Social Security number. When you do the taxes for your business, you'll then have to send a copy of each 1099 along with Form 1096 listing the total amount your business paid to independent contractors.

The Internal Revenue Service has tightened up its definition of when an individual performing work for a business is an employee, and when he or she is an independent contractor. If you have any doubts, contact your accountant or the Internal Revenue Service to clarify whether any individual performing work for your business is an employee or an independent contractor.

Technologically Speaking

◆

IF YOU were starting your home-based publishing business ten years ago, you probably could have managed with no more technology than a telephone and a no-frills personal computer. Today you may also need a high-speed Internet connection, scanner, fax machine, copier, cell and cordless phone, and voice mail. Many home-based publishing entrepreneurs who used to beg off getting a faster computer or a new computer program because they didn't have the time to learn to use it don't have that excuse. Even the most sophisticated software programs have a pretty short learning curve.

The technological advances that took hold in the late twentieth century now make it so easy to run a business that you may have twice as much time to do the things you started your home-based publishing business for—meeting with customers and creating products—because the computer is taking care of the grunt work. Now that you can dictate all kinds of documents into voice-recognition programs, you're free to perform other tasks for business owners—unless, that is, they decide to quit and start their own business.

Computers

ONCE UPON a time, when it came to your primary computer system, you had two choices: state of the art or price. Today, you can get both, along with as many special add-ons and features as you can cram onto a hard drive. But the technological advances in basic computer systems is dizzying: In 1996, having 1 gigabyte of storage space on your hard drive seemed like overkill to most people. Two years later, 4 gigs became the standard, at one-quarter of the price of its two-year-old predecessor.

With powerful computer systems readily available and very inexpensive, there is no excuse not to buy a system that has as much power as you can afford, which is probably a lot more than you need.

The first decision you'll have to make involves whether you want a PC or a Macintosh. For some people, the choice is political, for others it's practical, though the gap is narrowing every day when it comes to the difference between the two platforms. People used to be concerned with the ability to transfer files from one platform to another; now it's an issue of being able to find software for the Mac, since many software manufacturers no longer feel it's worth their while to produce cross-platform programs for what they feel is a minority segment of computer users.

The next decision concerns portability. Do you want your computer to be located primarily in your office, or do you think you'll need to take it with you? Some home-based publishing entrepreneurs want to have both, while others only need a desktop. Technology is one of those funny things where you don't know you need something until you try it out, and then once you get used to it, you wonder how you ever lived without it, it streamlines your life so. Though laptops do not have the storage capacity of their desktop counterparts, many people don't require huge hard drives in order to store very large files. The advantage laptops do have is that if you have to be out on the road on a regular basis taking notes, entering data directly onto a laptop the first time saves you from having to enter it again. Plus, if you need to demonstrate something to a customer or pull up some figures, the file is right there, and saves you from having to get back to the client later, therefore providing the client with a chance to change his or her mind. And if you need to check out some facts online, again, you can do it on the spot.

Some home-based publishing entrepreneurs invest the majority of their computer budget in a laptop, then get a less-powerful but much-less expensive desktop model for the office. This way, you have the best of both worlds.

In either case, it's a good idea to go with a well-known computer brand with a company that offers a decent warranty. Or you can visit a computer reseller in your area, usually a small shop and service company that builds computers to your specifications. If the company is available to answer questions relatively quickly and gives a warranty, many entrepreneurs prefer to go this route. Your time is too valuable once your business is up and running to waste time on the phone waiting for a technical support representative to help you with a problem.

Since computer standards and technology change so rapidly, you'll need to do your own research when it comes to suggesting how much RAM you need to run your business, as well as the size of your hard drive. Not only are everyone's needs different, according to their startup size as well as their industry and the software they'll use, but by the time you read this, any state-of-the-art specifications will already be obsolete. So do your own research and take advantage of the information to help you run your business more efficiently and effectively.

Printers

O N E O F the most often-made predictions at the dawn of the personal computer era turned out to be the most wrong: "The office of the future will be paperless." If your home-based publishing business turns out like most, you'll probably be buried in the stuff.

Who knows how this happened? No matter—it's quite probable that after your computer, your printer will turn out to be the most important piece of hardware you'll buy for your home-based publishing business. It's important to get the right fit. Here's what to look for.

INK JET PRINTERS

For most of the printing jobs you'll do at your new business, an ink jet printer is probably the best choice. Ink jets outsell lasers, in part because they print in colors as well as in black and white, and also because their text print quality is so crisp that it's virtually indistinguishable from laser printer output.

When selecting a printer, pay particular attention to the print quality, which traditionally is measured in dots per inch (dpi), also referred to as resolution. Most ink jets print from 30 to 720 dpi vertically and horizontally; some use special modes that require two passes through the printer—and therefore more time—to print at 1200 or even 1440 dpi.

However, dpi is not the only measure of quality you should look for in an ink jet printer. The speed of your printer, described as pages per minute (ppm), is also an important consideration. Ink jets have traditionally printed at a slower rate than lasers—two to four pages per minute as compared to the four to six ppm capability of a laser. However, ink jets are rapidly gaining ground.

The first ink jet printers required specially-treated paper to avoid fuzzy images, but thankfully that's no longer the case. Plain paper works well for most documents and images, although for important documents and photographs, you'll want to invest in special bright-white ink jet papers and photo papers.

LASER PRINTERS

If you're 100 percent sure you won't need to use color in the documents you produce yourself in the office, then you should spring for a laser printer. Besides being faster, laser printers produce documents with darker, sharper text; it's no wonder that "laser quality" is still the standard by which all other output from other printers is judged.

Laser printers print around four to six pages per minute, regardless of the amount of text or density of the images on the page, unlike an ink jet printer, which gets bogged down with an increase in text complexity and images. With laser printers, however, the amount of time it takes to print the first page is usually at least twice as long as for each subsequent pages, due to the time it takes for the computer to process and then send the digital image to the printer, so to speed things up you should look for a printer that claims to have a fast first-page printing time.

Plain paper works fine for most laser-printer jobs, but as with an ink-jet printer, for special jobs you may want to invest in higher-quality stock. Lasers have the added advantage of being able to print directly on labels, transparencies, card stock, and envelopes.

MULTIFUNCTION PERIPHERALS

If you want a printer to be more than just a printer, you should spring for a multifunction unit that not only prints but also sends and receives faxes, copies, and scans, and can also serve as a voice-mail center.

Multifunction peripherals usually use ink jet technology. They are appealing to business owners who don't want to clutter up a small office with four or more different pieces of electronic equipment when one would do it all, and do a good job, at that.

When multifunction devices first came out, they could only print in one color, but their ink jet roots now provide them with the capability of printing all the colors of the rainbow. More so than with the other machines, multifunction peripherals rely on sturdy paper-handling ability, since they will be used in a variety of ways. You should look for a sturdy paper-feed tray for originals, an ample tray for paper stock (100 sheets or more), and a good-size output tray. In case you run out of paper or ink, the ability to receive and maintain 20 or more pages in memory is crucial.

Overall, multifunction units are great if you don't have the space and don't need to use any one of the functions at great frequency. Otherwise, you should spring for a standalone machine that can handle heavy-duty jobs.

Scanners

SCANNERS ALLOW you to run an image or a document directly into its own file, where you can then edit the text and manipulate the graphic. Like printers, they work on a dots-per-inch standard and allow you to scan the image in order to catch a minimum of detail or to capture it as rich as you'd like.

Like printers, scanners have also experienced great technological advances. There are handheld scanners as well as flatbeds that work in much the same way as a copy machine does, but while the handheld models were once more affordable than flatbeds—but less accurate—today the flatbeds are your best bet in the office. A portable handheld model will work on the fly.

You'll need special software in order to first scan an image and then process it, but most of what you'll need comes bundled when you buy the scanner.

Software Selection: What Do You Want to Do Today?

THOUGH THE majority of computers today come loaded with more software than you'll probably ever use, it's likely that you'll need at least one kind of software that is specific to your home-based publishing business.

Much of the software you need to perform the simplest tasks—from writing letters to keeping track of your customer list—comes packaged together, so you only have to load one program in order to get three or more. Of course, you still have to load at least a number of floppy disks—or the contents of one CD—but the advantage of these bundled packages is that the programs are designed to work easily with each other, to transfer the contents of a word processing file seamlessly into a database program. Plus, it's cheaper to buy them all together than separately.

Many software manufacturers allow you to try before you buy by downloading a scaled-down version or a full-fledged version that turns into a pumpkin after a limited period of time. So if you're unsure whether a particular program can help to grow your business, see if you can try it for free first.

Here's a rundown of the different kinds of software you'll most likely need to run your business.

Word Processing

A word processing program allows you to manipulate words to create documents like letters, reports, even booklets. One of the greatest timesavers of word processing programs is the ability to merge fields from a database into a document, saving you from having to change the name, address, and salutation in each letter.

Spreadsheets

Spreadsheets are a kind of graphical calculator, which you can use to create financial charts of your revenue and expenses or inventory and keep track of as many different values as possible.

Accounting

Financial software allows your checkbook to come alive and integrate account information from inventory lists, price lists, invoices, customer files, anything imaginable. It will even print out your checks for you; all you have to do is sign them.

Database

Database software is similar to spreadsheet programs, except instead of processing numbers it processes names. You can sort your customer list alphabetically, by ZIP code, or by any other value you need.

Desktop Publishing

Once upon a time, home-based publishing entrepreneurs had to hire graphic artists to paste up art and copy for brochures, newsletters, and other promotional materials. The publishing software available today makes it possible for anyone to create materials that look like they came from a professional designer's light table, because the templates in these programs that make creating brochures as easy as cutting and pasting electronically were thought up by crackerjack graphic artists.

Graphics

You can create a pen-and-ink drawing, change the color of any picture, or airbrush a photograph with programs like Corel Draw and Photoshop. One click and your mouse becomes a calligraphy pen, a paintbrush, pencil, or whatever else you'd like to use.

Telecommunications

If you want to send a fax via computer, visit the Web, or send e-mail, you'll need to install software that can handle it. Most often, your gateway to the Internet—an Internet service provider (ISP) or one of the big guys like America Online—provides you with the software you need. To read and send e-mail, you'll need to get your own program which, again, you can download for free.

Voice Recognition

When it comes to the one technological development that might have appeared on *The Jetsons*, voice recognition software has got to be it. Essentially, you talk to your computer the way you might dictate letters. You can also give it commands such as print or stop, and it follows your orders.

To Network, or Not to Network?

AFTER EVERYONE in a given office got their first computers and became utterly dependent on them, the next obvious question concerned how a person in marketing could share a file or other information with a manager in production. Passing disks back and forth worked for awhile but got old fast. Home-based publishing business owners got tired of buying a printer for every computer. Why couldn't they just be linked together?

The solution arrived in the form of a network. If you plan to have at least one other person working with you in your business, you should seriously consider installing a computer network to streamline your work. Most people in an office occasionally need to share something, whether it's data, programs, printers, or hard drives. If the data you wish to share is not sensitive in nature and if the need to share occurs frequently enough, a small office network would be easier than swapping disks or desks.

The desire to share a printer is frequently the spark that starts a small business on the road to a network. After all, why equip three to ten computers with their own printers when, depending on the physical size and location of the office, you can set up a small network and share one or two printers within close proximity to the computers? The need to share information and computer files is another impetus for a small business owner to consider installing a network.

Before you decide whether or not to network your small business, you must first take a hard look at your data. Data should be classified as either sensitive or nonsensitive. Sensitive data is information that might cause harm to either the company or to employees of the company if the information were leaked or otherwise divulged. One example of sensitive data is payroll and accounts payable information. If your competition is aware of your accounts payable balances and history, they may undercut your prices or offer better terms to your customers. Or if an employee knows what you are paying your other employees, he or she can use that information to bargain for a pay raise. Employee appraisals are also among the most sensitive data maintained on a small business's computers. If you decide to place this type of data on a network, various methods exist to protect sensitive data.

Nonsensitive data is any information that is commonly and publicly available, or which can be easily obtained through methods besides hacking or breaking into the computer system. Your sales price list would be considered to be nonsensitive data.

Once you've decided to install a network, you need to determine which type of network is best. Though there are many types of networks available, for the small business just starting out, two in particular excel: serverless and server-based. They're relatively simple to maintain and to set up.

In a serverless network, each computer is connected to another in a line using coaxial cable. Besides the cable, you'll need a network card and a network-based software program—like Windows NT—and that's it. Each computer and/or user in the network is given a unique name and password in order to access the other hard drives linked together via the network. In a serverless network, no one computer controls the network and all shared resources are controlled by individual computers.

A server-based network differs in that one computer in the link, the server, controls the entire network. Most often, a server-based network contains either data that all networked users can access and is known as a file server, or acts as a queue for organizing print jobs before they are sent on to the printer. In this configuration, the server hosts all or the majority of the shared data or information; users log onto the server to access the necessary data. If there are confidentiality issues and employees don't want others to start nosing around their hard drives, a server-based network prevents this. A password and user name are required to access a server-based network.

Hooking up a server-based network is more complex than a serverless network, but a computer-savvy individual can do it with one of the comprehensive networking books on the market, a computer expert at a retail shop who can provide you with all of the network cards, cables, and software you need, and lots of patience.

Telephone Systems and Fax Machines

IT'S EASY to select the right phone system for your home-based publishing business, right? Even if you do most of your business over the phone with customers who are around the block or on the other side of the globe, your present one will work just fine, and as long as you answer your phone with your business name between the hours of nine and five, you're fine.

Try again. If you want to reap the revenue that other home-based publishing entrepreneurs do and you do a lot of business over the phone, you must first act like a real business. Otherwise, your customers and suppliers aren't going to treat you like a real business. Even if you're the sole employee of You, Inc., you'll need to rethink your phone approach, though that doesn't mean you'll have to spring for a complex multiline phone system, either.

The great thing about doing most of your business by phone is that, barring an up-and-running Internet connection, you can project a professional demeanor to your clients but be as comfortable as you want, whether that means working in your pajamas or outside in a hammock. First, you'll have to select the phone system that best fits your needs.

If you just want to receive and place phone calls—and nothing else—a single-line phone will work well. However, things are seldom that simple, even for a person who's working alone in a modest home office.

If you are working by yourself, you should get an additional phone line with your business number. Then use your home number—which probably isn't used much by other family members during the day—as your combination fax/Internet access line and the business line as your primary form of communication. Or else you can use the business line for incoming calls and the residential line for outgoing, since in most cases in-state toll calls are more expensive for a business than for a personal number.

For voice mail capabilities, you can use the services offered by your local phone company, buy a software system for your computer, or get a standalone unit with a receiver. The computer-based applications have multiple functions, including the ability to fax, and more advanced programs offer multiple mailboxes, paging, and call-forwarding choices. You can even tie incoming numbers to your database program so that when a customer calls, your computer instantly takes note and the customer's database information will appear on the screen before the second ring.

The downside to these more complex programs is that they're not only more expensive and difficult to set up, but your computer must remain on 24 hours a day. Standalone units work well, but often are limited in the services they offer. So are voice mail services offered by the phone company, but they have one big advantage, especially for entrepreneurs who live in areas where power surges and outages are common, rendering standalone units and computer-based software totally useless: They can still accept and process calls even if you've lost power.

If you have at least a few other people working in your office, you'll need something more powerful to transfer calls from one to another, as well as multiple mailboxes, not only for each employee but for company options, such as taking customer names, placing orders, and leaving general messages. The simplest but more costly solution is Centrex service, which is available from your local phone company. Centrex can install multiple phone lines and voice mail at several sites in the same state, in essence creating a single, seamless phone system.

A precursor to Centrex that is still used widely is a phone switch, also known as a PBX, or private branch exchange. PBX tends to be cheaper than Centrex but requires more maintenance to keep it up and running. A third option, and probably the most palatable if you're just starting out but need a multiple-user phone

line, is a hybrid system available from most phone network vendors that say they specialize in business solutions. These hybrids offer multiline phones in either analog or digital format in addition to voice mail. Many manufacturers offer hybrids, so it's easy to get the services you need at a reasonable price, along with responsive maintenance and troubleshooting.

As for fax machines, the choice of whether to use traditional thermal paper or plain paper is up to you. However, if you want to project a professional image for your business from the start, you'll need a dedicated fax line, or at least one that is shared with the number you typically use for Internet access. As discussed earlier, you may want to investigate the multifunction devices that incorporate fax, copying, and scanning capabilities. Just make sure that callers will be able to reach it directly and don't have to call you first to tell you to turn it on. Not only is this unprofessional, but it sends the wrong message to customers.

Finding Money for Your Home-Based Publishing Business

✦

YOU OFTEN hear interviews with top entrepreneurs and business owners who say, "I started with nothing and look where I am today." Yes, it's entirely possible to start your home-based publishing business on a single frayed shoestring and to build it into an international conglomerate. However, two things are frequently left unsaid in these stories: These successful founders worked their tails off and were as frugal as possible, but when their businesses started to take off, in most cases, they still acted as if there was little money in the bank. Success in business is determined less by how much you start out with, although that is indeed a crucial part, but more by how you handle what you get once your own home-based publishing business starts to take off.

Start-Up Costs

FOR MANY people, their idea of a business is governed by the companies they've worked for in the past. Unfortunately, it's this image that most often intimidates entrepreneurs who are just starting to get their own home-based publishing businesses off the ground: Either they think they need everything a larger, more established business has, from fancy networked telephone systems to a professionally-decorated office, and they spend way too much to open, or else they become over-whelmed by the amount of money they think they need to open their doors and never do so because they figure they'll never be able to come up with that kind of money.

Of course, the amount of money you'll need will vary depending on the type of business you're starting, but cer-tain across-the-board expenses apply to most small business startups. The good news is that it's probably a lot less than you think.

First, estimate what you'll need to present your business to your first cus-tomer. As a rule, service businesses require less money to start up because it's not necessary to tie up available cash in inventory. There are exceptions, however, and hooking up with distributors and wholesalers who will allow you to order parts and items as you need them—also known as just-in-time inventory—can help to minimize the amount of money you'll need to allocate toward startup costs.

Using your business plan as well as your own instincts, adapt the following list to chart the startup expenses for your home-based publishing business, either in terms of monthly payments or buying an item outright. If you already own the item—like a computer—put a zero in the

space; this means you'll have more money to spend in the other categories.

Overhead

Facility improvements/decorating

Computer

Other office equipment leases

Office supplies

Telephone/fax machine/voice mail

Office furniture

Product inventory

Business licenses and permits

Insurance

Advertising

Attorney fees

Accountant fees

Stationery, including business cards

Signs

Miscellaneous expenses

Once you've estimated your startup costs, decide whether you can cut corners anywhere. Can you use office equipment you already have? Is a state-of-the-art com-puter essential in the beginning, or can you borrow the year-old model that your brother-in-law no longer uses? Running a home-based publishing business is a continuous process of making choices between two or more options and figuring if the higher-priced model will give you more for your money or the lower-priced item provides real value while saving you a few bucks.

Figuring your budget in advance and deciding where you can cut corners is excellent practice for the day-to-day decisions you will encounter once you start your home-based publishing business.

If you are finding it difficult to come up with concrete figures, put your best bloodhound skills to work. If you've sent for information on a trade organization and have received it, go through the information, leaf through the magazine, go onto the Web site of vendors to check the prices on their online catalogs. And if you're having trouble making your list concise, remember the advice in Chapter 14 for scoping out your competitors. Do the same thing, but this time do it with an eye toward where they skimp and where they invest more money.

Feel free to revise your list as you collect more information and discover the areas where you can reduce your expenditures and where you'll need to budget more money.

Your Monthly Budget

IN THE course of running your home-based publishing business, you'll have to deal with not one but two budgets: one for your business and one for yourself.

Your home-based publishing business budget, or operating budget, differs from the schedule you drew up for your startup costs for several reasons. After operating your business for even a short time, you'll have a much better idea of where the money goes, as well as what comes in. You'll also have some sense of when the money tends to arrive in your bank account, so you'll know when you can expect to be able to pay your bills.

Essentially, a budget is a projection of the revenue, and expenditures, and subsequent profit, frequently offered in detail on a month-by-month basis and, in more general terms, over a year's time. An operating budget should provide a home-based publishing entrepreneur with a sense of discipline when it comes to spending the business's money. In a way, an operating budget provides an at-a-glance snapshot to allow you to see how your projections are panning out and where adjustments—if any—are necessary.

For instance, your fixed costs can't be changed, but if you're working hard and still aren't generating enough cash to cover all of your expenses each month, a quick glance at your budget will allow you to make one of several choices:

+ Increase sales by raising your prices, selling more to each customer, expanding your market range.

- ✦ Cut expenses by opting for part-time rather than full-time help, or by reducing nonfixed costs.
- ✦ Allow more time for the market to become aware of you, then even more time for customers to decide to make a purchase.

None of these are easy choices, of course. But developing and then keeping track of your operating budget will help secure a great future for your business and yourself.

Overhead

Salary

Insurance

Telephone line

Fax line

Credit card commissions

Postage

Stationery

Office supplies

Printing

Advertising

    Mailing list rentals

    Mailing house services

Miscellaneous marketing fees

Professional Expenses

Trade association dues and memberships

Accountant fees

Attorney fees

Independent contractor fees

Office Equipment

Copier leases

Computers

Printers

Software

Company Vehicle(s)

Loan/lease payment

Registration

Insurance

Gas

Repairs/maintenance

Employee Expenses

Payroll

Taxes

Insurance

Workers' compensation

Bonuses

Employee discounts

Although this is a book about starting a home-based publishing business, it's equally important to keep tabs on the money you spend on the personal side of the ledger. If you have never kept a budget for your personal life, now is the perfect time to start. You'll have to account and keep track of every penny that you spend in your business; doing the same thing when it comes to your personal life will help you to manage your money better overall. Plus it means you'll have more money to invest back into your business; people who stick to a budget tend to not fritter away their money, later wondering where it all went.

It's a good idea to prepare two personal budgets: one for how you live now and one to project into your personal life once you have started your business. For instance, once you start working at your own business full-time, you may decide that you no longer need to spend $400 a month on new clothes, especially if you're going to be working at home by yourself, while the amount you budget for lunches out may be totally eliminated in your personal budget but will jump in your business budget. If you need to entertain current and potential clients over lunch, part of your restaurant tab can be treated as a business deduction; check with your

accountant to see just what percentage you can deduct.

Personal Budget

Housing

Utilities (gas, electric, phone)

Food

Car payment

Car expenses

Credit card payments

Entertainment

Savings

New clothes

Lunches out

Miscellaneous

Now add it up. Where can you comfortably cut expenses?

Terms of Endearment

IT MAY seem that you're spending a lot of time learning basic business lingo, and that's fine. As you continue to read, apply these basics to the real-world situations you think you will encounter when running your own home-based publishing business. After all, you're more likely to be able to negotiate favorable terms with clients and convince a banker to give you a loan if you use terms that everyone understands.

Within the information you detail in your budget and then use to project where changes are needed is everything you'll need to draw up documents that are essential to your business. Whether drawn up in plain-text format or spreadsheet, the numbers will help to dictate the steps you should take next. They are:

+ Sales forecasts
+ Cash flow projections
+ Balance sheet
+ Income statement, also known as profit and loss statement

Sales Forecasts

TRYING TO predict future sales is an inexact science at best, even for long-term entrepreneurs. For home-based publishing entrepreneurs who are just getting their feet wet, it can be downright maddening. How can you possibly predict your sales volume for the first month of business, let alone a year down the road, when so many variables affect it, along with your entrepreneurial inexperience?

The easiest—and most accurate—way to forecast future sales is with a simple chart that provides three different figures:

+ Pie-in-the-sky figures, or what number would be beyond your wildest dreams

but still within the realm of the type of business you're running, your location, your time commitment, etc.

+ Catastrophic figures, or the amount of sales you could expect to make if a flood, earthquake, and fire occurred all in the same month

+ Somewhere in between, which most likely is the number you get by adding up the two previous figures and then dividing by two

Keep in mind that as the months fly by and you gain more experience running your business, you'll also start to learn about the realistic figures you can expect. But it's fun to dream and to have a goal. Regarding the pie-in-the-sky number, what would you have to do differently in your business in order to even come close to this figure? Ask yourself this question as you run your business, and one day you may just reach these lofty heights.

CASH FLOW PROJECTIONS

Cash flow is the lifeblood of a business, since it symbolizes the steady movement of cash in and out of a business. With a cash flow projection, you'll be able to keep tabs on when you expect to receive revenue or money owed to you by your customers and manage this money so it is available when you need it to pay your bills. Getting the numbers down in writing will help you figure which months you should stockpile extra cash—perhaps by postponing that renovation project you had planned—and when you'll have enough revenue flowing into your checking account to reschedule it. Or you can plan to hold a special sale for the months when you believe you'll have more money going out than coming in; the discount you provide to your customers is worth it if your cash flow is positive instead of negative.

Unlike a traditional ledger or balance sheet, with a cash flow projection and statement you can include deductions for depreciation and amortization. Although cash-flow projections could arguably be used to prove that your home-based publishing business isn't doing so hot—after all, if you didn't include the depreciation on your computer and business vehicle in the projections, your cash flow would look great—as is the case with comparing the accrual accounting method with a cash accounting system, the diligent use of cash flow statements and projections provides a much more accurate picture of the financial health of your business.

Balance Sheet

A balance sheet is another important form of financial statement for your home-based publishing business, but unlike the others, sales projections and monthly revenue are not factors.

Instead, a balance sheet is designed to indicate the net worth of a business,

including any and all assets as well as liabilities. Assets are listed as both current assets, such as accounts receivable, inventory, and all office supplies, and fixed assets, which include the full value of business real estate, office equipment (owned outright or leased), and fixtures. Current and fixed assets are added together to provide the total assets owned by the company.

Liabilities are listed as current (accounts payable, taxes that are due, and any other loans or debts that are coming due over the next year) and long-term (mortgages, multiple-year vehicle leases, and contractual agreements with other businesses or independent contractors with whom you have signed a contract for a term longer than one year).

A balance sheet is normally prepared on a quarterly basis for the first year you're in business, then once a year after that.

Income Statement

An income statement is a simple document that can be prepared in a single keystroke with one of the bookkeeping software programs that can also prepare invoices, balance your checkbook, and print out checks. An income statement, also known as a profit and loss statement, shows all given revenue over a stated period of time and all actual expenses, those that require cash to flow out of your business. Subtract the total expenses from the total revenue, and you are left with either a profit or a loss, not including any business tax you must pay (payroll taxes are included in your income statement as an operating expense). Subtract the business tax, and you are left with a net profit or a net loss.

An income statement should be prepared at least once a month to keep track of the health of your home-based publishing business.

Finding the Funds You Need

MONEY IS the oil that greases the squeaky wheel of American business, large and small. While the primary ingredient of small-business success is hard work, and lots of it, money is still essential to launching and then maintaining the often-spotty first year of its history.

Now that you have a good idea of how much money you need to start your home-based publishing business, and how much you'll need to generate to pay the bills every month, how are you going to find it? You're a true entrepreneur if you believe your talents and energy are so wide-reaching that the cash will start pouring in—and never let up—from the first week that you're open for business, but even if this fairy tale were to come true, there are far too many contingencies

and unexpected expenses to be able to comfortably rely on this for long.

One way to finance your business is to use available cash as it comes in, a kind of pay-as-you-go method. The problem with this method is that if you're forced to rely on whatever comes in, or whatever's left over after you cover the basic expenses for your business and for your personal life, your business growth can be sporadic, or nonexistent and unpredictable.

Steady business growth relies on consistent effort and marketing, and if you plan such a big advertising campaign one month, you won't have the money to advertise again for six months, your customers and clients-to-be may wonder where you've gone during your hiatus, and some may think you've gone out of business, calling a competitor before they think to contact you first. Remember the tortoise: Slow and steady wins the race, not rabbit-like unpredictable bursts.

There are a variety of ways to find the capital you need for your new enterprise. Many new business owners use their own funds, by liquidating savings accounts, stocks, bonds, and other investments, selling a house or another big-ticket item. While this may limit the projects and growth of a small home-based publishing business, the advantage is that because you're not pressured by outside investors or the need to meet a monthly bank loan payment, you answer only to yourself and your own vision for your business, not what outsiders who may not be familiar with the quirks of your business dictate to you.

Of course, you can also build up your personal credit by using it to lease or rent the equipment you need to start your business. Leasing a computer or a vehicle means that more cash will be freed up for the day-to-day expenses of running your business, and can buy you time to establish your business and win over a reluctant customer who wants to make sure you'll be around in six months to complete the project. If you choose this route, try to insert the name of your business into the lease documents. That way, you're taking a step toward establishing credit in the name of your business only. It can be difficult to get a corporate credit card or business lease when you're first starting out; establishing a business checking account is easy, however, and will help future creditors examine the financial record of your home-based publishing business.

Another way to personally finance your business is to take advantage of the assets you've already built up, without selling them, by using your personal credit cards to buy business equipment and/or get cash advances, by taking out a home equity loan, or by getting a second mortgage.

A surprisingly large number of entrepreneurs raise at least part of the capital for startup and operating expenses by asking friends, family, and previous business colleagues to lend a hand. Though some creditors may ask for partial ownership in your fledgling firm, most will probably be satisfied by your personal guarantee of a payback date—with interest—despite what happens with your business.

Though you may be the most enthusiastic person in the world when it comes to your home-based publishing business, many people will want to know about your own financial commitment to the business before they invest anything. To some it may not matter; most people will want to know that you're at least willing to take a financial risk with some of your own assets before they will provide your business with capital.

Though it may sometimes seem like banks and other financial institutions are just waiting for you to show up, give your five-minute spiel, and then cheerfully write you a check for whatever amount you want to start your new business, the truth is that given their federal ties and restrictions, they will probably be reluctant to loan you money until you have a decent track record to show that yours is a viable business. Even then, they may require a significant chunk of collateral to safeguard their investment.

Banks are more likely to give you a personal loan, even though you will use it for business purposes. It definitely helps if you already have an established relationship with a bank for your personal accounts; you may want to ask for a small loan in the name of your home-based publishing business that you can pay back in one year. Once you have established a record of prompt payments with your business, the bank may be more likely to loan you larger amounts or provide you with a line of credit you can draw against as needed.

The Small Business Administration also has numerous guaranteed loan programs available to small businesses, even startups, but these tend to be associated with banks, so you still have to apply through banks.

Of course, arranging for customers to pay upfront—while providing a small discount—will help improve the cash flow of any business. You'll need to gauge your business, customers, and how much you are likely to generate from this technique, and whether it's worth it to provide the discount.

Venture capitalists and other equity investors are in the headlines when it comes to many of the high-tech or other companies that grow 1,000 percent or more each year, but for the great majority of small, usually one-person companies that don't expect to gross more than a million dollars in the first year, and who need a lot less than a seven-figure sum in order to start, venture capital is a whole other galaxy. Venture capital and private angel investors look for fast growth and incredible double-digit

returns on their money in a short period of time. The bad news is that these investors typically request a sizable ownership chunk—25 percent to 51 percent usually—and somewhere down the road, if they don't agree with the way you're growing your company, they'll unceremoniously boot you out. As a rule, the number of businesses they agree to fund is ridiculously low. Many get bombarded with thousands of business plans each year; they may invest in only a few can't-lose companies. Most home-based publishing entrepreneurs will never need to turn to a venture capitalist.

How much are you willing to risk in order to start your business? If you're like many Americans, you're probably long on debt and possessions but short on savings. If your heart skipped a beat when you first saw the total amount you think you need to start your business, there are a number of other options. Some are more drastic than others, but remember, running a business is a risky venture. You'll have to take risks every day in the course of doing business. You might as well find out now just how badly you want to start your business by seeing whether any of the following options make sense to you.

EXTENDING CREDIT TO CUSTOMERS

If you want to start a business where you collect payment before you have to provide a product or service to your customers, you can skip this section. Most retail businesses conduct pay-as-you-go transactions. Customers can choose to not pay up front by using a credit card; however, interest charges make their purchase more expensive.

Most home-based publishing businesses are service-oriented enterprises, so it's standard for customers to pay for something after they order, and possibly long after they receive it. The collection industry is growing by leaps and bounds, and not just by negotiating with consumers to pay a long-ignored credit card bill, either. You may end up chasing some customers all the way into small claims court or employing an attorney who specializes in collections.

Most business owners with lapsed accounts do not do this deliberately; once you start your home-based publishing business, you'll find that unexpected turns and twists in the entrepreneurial road can quickly turn your dreams of great success into scrambling to keep the light bill paid. Therefore, a customer's priority to pay you may be low on *his* list.

Again, it depends on the type of company you run, but when you're working with a new customer, it makes sense for service-oriented businesses—where net 30 is the rule—to try to collect 50 percent of the total fee before work commences. Then you can bill again after you complete the project.

Better yet is to arrange to bill a client's credit card in installments. That way, you're more likely to be paid in full. The speed of payment may be worth the few percentage points you need to pay the credit card company for the privilege of merchant status. In fact, since many Americans use plastic for almost everything imaginable—many pay it off in full each month—it's worth your while to investigate being qualified to accept MasterCard, Visa, and American Express. The more choices you provide to your customers, the easier it will be for them to pay you, and the more likely they will choose you over a competitor.

How Much of a Monetary Risk Are You Willing to Take?

WHEN YOU start your own home-based publishing business, it's very likely that you'll have to get used to a drastically lower income, at least in the beginning.

In your notebook, ask yourself the following questions before you quit your job to start a business.

+ How much money have you budgeted to live on during the launch of your business and afterward?

+ Do you think of yourself as a risk-taker?

- ✦ If you suddenly had to get used to living at a level one-third to one-half of what you do now, could you?

- ✦ With your loss of salary and job title comes a loss of status. Do you see it as a threat if you don't have a job that you and others can identify with?

- ✦ What will your immediate family think? Will your decision to accept a lower salary put a crimp in any of their plans?

Borrowing Money

THE ISSUE of borrowing money in these credit-weary days is apt to be a sticky one among entrepreneurs who may have taken out a loan to finance their businesses. "I'm in enough debt already," you may say, "Why would I want to borrow any more?"

As you'll see, sometimes your cash flow won't keep up with your expenses. Even if you and/or a partner holds down a steady job, there will be times when even that won't be enough. Operating a home-based publishing business can eat up huge amounts of cash, and it may be necessary to borrow money.

If you have a rich relative or a sizable trust fund, you can skip over this section. But if you're like most of us, you'll need a conventional financing source. Since you already know to anticipate these cycles, especially if your business has sharp peaks

and valleys throughout the year, you should take steps now to line up an available source of credit that you can draw on immediately.

I know of many examples where entrepreneurs have drawn on their credit cards to initially finance their business, and then have gone back to them when things got slow. At anywhere from a 12 to 21 percent annual rate of interest, this is definitely an expensive way to borrow money. Even if you fully intend to pay it back before interest has a chance to accumulate, there will be times when you are only able to make the minimum payment.

Some entrepreneurs form partnerships solely for this reason: to have a silent partner with deep pockets who's looking for a good rate of return on his money. But if you prefer to have a partner for other reasons—or to go it alone—and you don't want to have to rely on your credit cards, there is another option, and that is to open a line of credit at your bank.

If you don't want to go this route—or get turned down for it—there is the old-fashioned way, and that is to save for a rainy day. When business is booming and revenue is strong, set aside a certain percentage—some say 20 percent of every check that comes in—and sock it away in an interest-bearing savings account. Don't invest it in a place where you don't have instant access to your funds—even though the interest rate may be better, you'll probably have to pay a penalty for early withdrawal from an IRA, mutual fund, or other investment. A money market fund is best; the interest rates tend to be a little higher than a passbook savings account, and you have immediate access to your money.

How to Raise Additional Capital

BECAUSE THE revenue from your business will be sporadic at times, many home-based publishing entrepreneurs turn to other sources of income. If you need to raise additional capital to finance your business, you may want to turn to parents or relatives. Some people rely on the proceeds from the sale of their house and move to an area where they can live mortgage-free in order to plow all the revenue from the business back into the business.

You have to be creative to stay in business these days, regardless of your venture. The advantage of other services that you offer is that many of them will result in additional business for your company, thus bringing your efforts full circle.

Improving Cash Flow

EVEN THOUGH the cash flow in your business may be erratic, you can

usually predict when it will slow down and when it will be high. This will help you to see which months you should stockpile some of your excess cash in order to provide you with cash flow and income in the down times.

Cash flow is defined as the pattern of movement of cash in and out of a business: revenue and expenses. If you apply for a loan with a bank or other financial company after your business is up and running, you'll have to provide an analysis of your cash flow; if you're just starting out, you may be required to provide the loan officer with a projected cash flow statement.

Cash flow includes all actual monies coming in and going out of the business, as well as cash, checks, and income from credit cards. Depreciation of your computer and other office equipment does not factor into your cash flow analysis.

The first step to improving your cash flow is to increase your business year-round. But the effects from this aren't always immediate, and there are things you can do to even out your cash flow a little more.

Tying in with your own cash flow projections, you might want to conduct special promotions designed to pull in more business during those times of the year when your cash flow needs boosting the most. For instance, you should plan to mail promotional offers to past customers in your slow months. Or you can send out direct mail packages offering your new products and services to past and present customers as well as those who have never purchased anything from you but have inquired about your business in the past.

Another way to even out your expenses and improve your cash flow is to ask your utility companies to average out your payments so that you pay the same amount each month year-round. And as I suggested earlier, if you stash away 20 percent of your gross revenue during the busy times, you'll have money to draw on during the slow months.

CHAPTER SIXTEEN

Day In, Day Out

✦

WHEN IT comes time to start to utilize the vast array of resources that are available to help you get your home-based publishing business up and running, one of the best ways to begin is to dive headfirst into it all. This chapter discusses the many experts, resources, and groups you can draw on to help make your business as strong as it can be.

Trade Associations

AS IS OFTEN said, it's not what you know, it's who you know. Membership in a variety of business associations can help you start your business and get ahead. A trade association can provide invaluable contacts as well as advice from people who have been running a business in your industry for a long time.

Membership is up in many professional industry organizations and business trade associations, so you'll have access to plenty of experts and mentors. In addition, organizations that focus on a variety of specific issues that you'll deal with in your business—whether it's computers, producing specialty foods, or owning a retail store—exist both on a national and regional basis, with state chapters of the large organizations as well as individual specialty groups. For example, I belong to the Vermont/New Hampshire Direct Marketing Association, a group of direct marketing professionals who meet every four weeks for a luncheon, talks, discussion, and networking. I've found that these meetings bring the issues that are often frequent discussions in business magazines to life so that you can surmise whether they'll work for you.

I recommend that you join an association that covers your industry in addition to one of the more general publishing trade associations. Most associations publish a regular newsletter, sell literature that covers specific aspects of their industry, and hold conventions where members can network, attend workshops, and visit trade show exhibitors who sell products that are pertinent to the field. Some associations also offer their members consultation services at reduced rates, credit-card acceptance privileges through a clearinghouse, health insurance, and long distance and toll-free number services at a discount. Though yearly membership rates can be high—up to $200 a year—most entrepreneurs report that membership is worth it because of all the benefits, networking, and ideas they receive to help them enhance their own businesses.

In addition to the national trade associations, there are many regional, statewide, and local organizations that home-based publishing entrepreneurs can join as well. These usually benefit small business owners by providing local marketing opportunities as well as reliable feedback. Some of the smaller associations were started by local members of a particular national organization who met through the national association, talked regularly on their own, and decided to form their own chapter. Some entrepreneurs start their own associations for their trade.

Consultants

ALMOST AS quickly as new businesses have been popping up all over the country, consultants have appeared to help novice entrepreneurs do their homework before they start a business and established business owners work out problems. These consultants speak at conventions, hold seminars, or offer one-on-one meetings. In many cases, consultants have also written extensively in their field, either now or in the past, so they have plenty of first-hand experience to draw on. Some consultants can also hook you up with another home-based publishing entrepreneur for whom you can work as an intern to see whether you're sure that you want to enter the business.

New seminars and conventions for aspiring and experienced publishing entrepreneurs are scheduled all over the country on a regular basis. The best way to find one in your area is to check the notices and advertisements in the publications produced by your national and regional business and communications associations, as well as the independently-owned publications for the publishing trade.

Training Courses

MANY TRADE associations and consultants who specialize in the publishing industry also hold workshops solely for entrepreneurs who are just getting started in their fields. Community colleges, adult schools, and computer centers often offer a wide variety of home-based publishing business courses as part of their regular schedules.

To find out about courses, write to or call community schools, trade organizations, and consultants, and ask to be placed on their mailing lists so you can be alerted to upcoming workshops and seminars. Most courses last a few intensive days and provide a condensed, birds-eye view of the business. Some involve strictly sit-down classroom learning, while others require you to conceptualize your home-based publishing business as well as your business plan over the course of a few days. This kind of workshop usually begins on a Friday and doesn't let up until Sunday afternoon.

Magazines and Trade Journals

AGAIN, MANY of the business and trade associations that cover your industry publish specialized magazines or newsletters that address the many topics that concern their members, as well as recently passed legislation and tax information that will affect the publishing industry. There are independent journals as well. Write to the industry-specific trade associations to find out about them.

The Small Business Administration

THE SMALL Business Administration, which you help to pay for with your tax dollars, is a veritable gold mine of information if you want to start your own home-based publishing business. There are three major divisions within the Small Business Administration that can assist you in the startup phase of your business, as well as provide you with advice and assistance once your business is up and running.

One is the Small Business Development Center, which counsels entrepreneurs in every conceivable type of business and at every level of development. The SBDC will set you up in private sessions with an entrepreneur who has experience in your field. There, you can ask about any phase of your business that you'd like, from marketing to locating suitable financing and how to keep the business going in tough times.

The SBA also runs the Small Business Institute on a number of college campuses nationwide. Each SBI tends to specialize in a given field, from engineering to business management, so if you're looking for very specific information, contact the nearest SBI that has the program you want. The assistance at an SBI is largely provided by students in the program, under the watchful eye of a professor or administrator.

The Service Corps of Retired Executives (SCORE) can be an exciting place for you to get information about your business. SCORE officers provide one-on-one counseling with retired business people who volunteer their time to help entrepreneurs like you get the help you need. Each volunteer counselor has extensive experience in a particular field and is eager to share his or her insights. SCORE also offers a variety of seminars and workshops on all aspects of business ownership that aspiring business publishers can attend; here, you'll get specific advice about the nuts and bolts of running a business in general, from bookkeeping to taxes.

As I mentioned in Chapter 15, the Small Business Administration loans money to small businesses, but you have to apply through a bank. The SBA then kicks in some of the funds and serves to guarantee your loan, based on your business plan. The SBA also offers a large variety of helpful booklets and brochures on all aspects of running a business.

To locate the SBA and its programs, look in the white pages of the phone book under United States Government. Call the office nearest you for information about the programs and services they provide locally.

To contact the SBA in Washington, write to:

The Small Business Administration
409 Third Street SW
Washington, DC 20416

Or call the SBA answer desk, 800-827-5722. You can also visit the SBA on line at www.sba.gov.

Tracking Your Progress

IN SOME cases, it may be pretty difficult to know in advance how quickly you'll progress in your home-based publishing business, and what form it will take. But if you draw up a plan in advance you'll be able to check your progress every week or month and adjust accordingly.

If you're like me and tend to underestimate the amount of time it will take you to accomplish a certain task, do yourself a favor and deliberately overestimate. One of your aims in running your new business should be to find your natural rhythm of working. Frequently, the frenzied pace at which we are accustomed to handling work tends to obscure the depths we can reach in our work. And if you're the type who enjoys checking items off your priority list more than doing the actual tasks themselves, look to your business as a way to begin to enjoy work for its own sake, and not to earn a gold star on your mental chart.

Getting and Staying Professional

SOMETIMES IT may seem difficult to maintain a professional image while you're working at home, in comfortable clothes, perhaps even in your pajamas. This is why many entrepreneurs choose to stick to a regular schedule and even get dressed up when they're working at home. Here are some suggestions you can implement to build an image of professionalism in your home office.

Maintain a separate phone line for business calls. Don't run extension phones off your business line into other areas of the house. Don't let your kids answer if you're off in another corner of the house. The phone should be used for business purposes only.

Be in the office at a set time each day and accomplish what you set out to do. People who work at home not only tend to work more hours than their office coun-

terparts, but they also are usually able to work for several hours at a stretch without interruption, which would be impossible in most office settings. If your business allows it, work during those times of the day or night when you are most productive. For instance, if you're a night owl, you can work until 2 a.m. Or if your mind is clearest first thing in the morning, start and end your work day early.

Some people look forward to working at home because they don't have to spend a half hour or more each morning just to look presentable. Just think of the time you'll save! Unfortunately, an awful lot of people think that working in their pajamas is akin to lolling around the house on a lazy Saturday afternoon and their productivity suffers. If you are one of them, you just may have to make believe that you're commuting and dress accordingly. Indeed, there are a number of people who, although they may not dress up as much as they would if they were going into the office for the day, which may just mean forgetting about the mascara or wearing sneakers with their suit, still dress differently for working at home than if they were *not* working at home.

Animals in Your Home Office

YOU MAY not have thought to consider the issue of having a cat or dog hang out with you while you work, but if you are a pet owner, believe me, the issue will come up. Perhaps you'll deal with it simply. Maybe the cat has already thrown up in the printer, or the dog jumped up on your lap and knocked your coffee into the computer keyboard. So from simple experience, you'll close the door to keep out not only your kids and neighbors, but also your pets.

For many of you, however, it'll be different. You're stuck at home working, and if you don't have employees, you may feel a bit lonely. You don't want human company, but a living breathing *something* in the room might be nice, especially if it does nothing more than sleep.

I've always had my six cats by my side when I'm sitting at the computer or sitting on the sofa writing longhand. It helps me keep my work rhythm, and they're usually content not to have your full attention if you're not paying attention to another human.

However, when you're on the phone, they might cause trouble, such as walking on the keyboard before you've had a chance to save that important report you've worked on all morning, or even stepping on the phone to disconnect you. Of course, these are all accidents, but they do happen. Still, I do find that cats are the perfect companion to get me into the groove of working.

Of course there are drawbacks. When I bring my computer to be serviced once

a year, my computer technician always asks if a mouse has been living in the computer, since he always pulls big clumps of gray fur from around the hard drive. Cats and dogs can be insistent, and sometimes when I sit on the sofa and talk on the cordless and one of my cats is nearby, she will not hesitate to let me know by vocalizing that she is unhappy that I have stopped petting her. Customers usually ask if I have a baby, but I say, no, it's a cat. Although you may find this explanation to be awkward if you're trying to convey a professional image, one unexpected benefit is that this usually helps to break the ice.

Taking a Break

WHENEVER YOU work for someone else in an office, even though you may not take an official coffee break, chances are that your entire workday is punctuated by interruptions—co-workers chatting, the phone, running errands, going to meetings—that keep you from working too long on one thing. This is both a good and bad thing—the breaks help to keep your mind fresh, but they can also prevent you from getting much done.

The lack of breaks that occur when you work from home is largely what accounts for the increased productivity that many home-based publishing entre- preneurs report. However, the downside is that you need occasional breaks in your day to relax your focus and give you a chance to recharge.

One way to take a break is to vary the kinds of work that you plan to do each day. Write for an hour or two, then make a few phone calls before you leaf through a couple of new business magazines that came out that week.

Another important way to take a break is to get away from your work, whether it's heading to the kitchen for a cup of tea or going outside for a walk. Even 15 minutes will do it. If you don't need to be by the phones constantly, you may even want to take a long lunch hour and eat at the local coffee shop, then pick up a few groceries or the dry cleaning on the way back.

Some home-based publishing entre- preneurs also take a break by exercising. Granted, it's easier to exercise regularly when you're working from home than on the days when you're in the office because you probably won't have to fight locker- room gridlock and the post-aerobic traffic jam in the shower.

If your schedule is flexible, you can take your lunch early or later in order to avoid the crowds. However, many entre- preneurs say that even a quick walk around the block is enough for them to clear their heads or give them some per-

spective on a particular problem that had been bothering them all morning.

No matter what your reasons are for taking a break, the important thing is that you indeed do it. If you don't, the dearth of built-in interruptions in a home-based publishing entrepreneur's life means that you may burn out on your work.

Balancing Your Home and Work Life

WHEN IT comes to the topic of working in the same place that you live, you'll probably get one of two reactions: "That sounds great" or "Ugh, that would be awful." Rarely do you find a person who is neutral about the topic of working at home. Sometimes, however, a negative reaction is due to the fact that a person's current studio apartment is crammed to the hilt already, which would leave no room for a home office. For other people, the problem lies in the belief that home is for the personal side of life, and they have no desire to let business permeate their domestic walls.

Some people will not be convinced that it's actually possible to combine work and home under one roof—*theirs*. For everyone else who is interested in the concept but needs a little guidance in how to mesh the two successfully, here's some help.

The first thing you need to do is to do is to make sure that there is a distinct line between your home office and your living space. If this isn't possible, for instance, if your at-home workspace is the dining room table, try to gather your work into a box or closet at the end of each workday, and especially on the weekends.

Then you need to set small goals for yourself and reward yourself when you've completed them. For instance, promise yourself that when you finish working on a report, you'll take a walk around the block. Things like that balance your home and work life so that your living space doesn't just turn into a workspace.

Half-Time Analysis

AFTER YOU'VE been running your own home-based publishing business for awhile, usually after a couple of months, it's a good idea to evaluate the areas where you've met or exceeded your goals and the areas where you would like to do a little better. Then adjust your workstyle accordingly and decide whether you want to continue working this way for the foreseeable future. A close analysis at this stage will focus your attention on the areas where you feel you fall short or concentrate on the parts that you enjoy most and do best at.

Performing this half-time analysis will also help you to decide how you're going to change your workstyle from that point on, if at all. So be honest and answer the following questions in your notebook in detail.

1. Do you feel that you've accomplished the main goals that you set out to do? How so?

2. List the five best things you've learned about your work and yourself as a result of running your own business and describe how you learned them.

3. List the five things you didn't learn but wanted to. How would you change your day-to-day operations to place more priority on them?

4. What do you want to do differently from now on, if anything? What do you want to remain the same?

5. What are you going to do now with what you've learned?

What If You Feel Isolated?

ONE OF the most common complaints that entrepreneurs have in making the adjustment to their new lives is the loss of face-to-face contact with other people. Here are seven ways to help relieve your feelings of isolation.

1. Get in touch with other entrepreneurs, whether they're in the publishing busi-

ness or not. Also check to see who else in your neighborhood is working from home. Most people who work from home won't take kindly to being interrupted during the day to participate in what may resemble a kaffeeklatsch, so you might want to make an informal contact and then offer to have both of you keep your options open. For instance, you may want to offer to accept a neighbor's express mail packages on the days when he has to be out of town, and he may ask you for tips on the best way to get a contract from your company. Don't push it, however, especially if you sense that a particular person is not crazy about the idea of socializing with other people who work from their home. For this reason, I think your best shot is with other entrepreneurs in your field.

2. Take a break by going online. There are a variety of working-from-home forums where you can find solutions to your problems of isolation as well as even give some advice to others who are going through what you've already dealt with. Sometimes, these sessions can even turn into fruitful working relationships.

3. One advantage of being a home-based publishing entrepreneur is that you're not required to be in your home office for every minute from nine to five. This means that you don't have to save up all your aggravating errands—like running to the dry cleaners or taking your dog to the vet—for Saturday, when it seems like everyone in the neighborhood has the same thing in mind. You can look to these errands as a way to beat your feelings of isolation. Once you visit the supermarket or dry cleaner during the day for a few weeks in a row, the people who work there will start to recognize you and chat with you.

4. If you regularly took an exercise class when you worked for somebody else, try to do the same thing when you're working from home. This may be a good case for involving other home-based entrepreneurs in your neighborhood. Find someone to go for a walk or a swim with at lunchtime.

5. Set up a network of other entrepreneurs in your industry for an e-mail round robin, or join an existing mailing list. In an e-mail round robin, someone poses a question or problem, and everyone gets to offer their two cents on the subject. After awhile, there are no questions asked, just an ongoing series of advice and comments. The fact that the members of the group live hundreds or thousands of miles away from each other doesn't matter.

6. Call your local chamber of commerce and find out if they have a group of

members who are home-based entrepreneurs and who meet regularly.

7. Establish a regular schedule, then stick to it. Nothing causes the feeling of isolation to grow more than nonstop work. People who live by themselves are especially prone to this. Unless you have regular overtime, when five o'clock arrives, try as hard as you can to leave the office and close the door. Then get out of the house and go where there are other people around.

Developing the Discipline

I T ' S   N O T easy for many people to set the alarm, get up, get dressed, and head for the computer instead of heading for a long commute. But once they sit down in front of the computer, they forget where they are and are able to concentrate fully on the work before them.

It may be hard to believe, but there are actually some people out there who decide that they don't want to run their own home-based publishing businesses after all, and so return to working in the office full-time. In some cases, they find that they just weren't able to learn to let go and enjoy being untethered from the office. Others may have found it difficult to recreate a ritual around working at home.

Troubleshooting

I T ' S   A   H A R D thing to admit that the extensive business plan you pondered, planned, and worked on for so long somehow isn't working out like you had thought. Should you keep plodding on and hope that it gets better? Or should you scrap your plans entirely?

Of course, you should realize that working from home may look very different than what you expected. So if what you're doing doesn't feel quite right, you should ask yourself if your initial expectations for your business were too high. Most of us have had a project we worked on that didn't live up to what we had expected. In that case, we try and figure out what went wrong, write it off, and try again.

If you're running your own business, however, you really don't have much time to waste on figuring out why it's not working. After all, you're supposed to be working. If your work falls off because you're trying to figure out another approach to being an entrepreneur, your clients may decide that you're not the right kind of business for them to direct work toward.

The first thing you have to do is determine where things have gone awry. Ask yourself the following questions:

✦ Did you over- or underschedule your time?

✦ Did you expect too much?

✦ Did it take you so long to get used to working from home that you never hit your stride?

✦ Did you decide to start your own business based not on your own desires, but somebody else's? Or what you *thought* you wanted, and not what would truly work for you?

✦ Are you working all the time?

If any of your answers indicate that you need to revamp your daily routine, then do it. Sometimes people who run their own businesses get so excited about it that they actually can't stop working.

Being a home-based publishing entrepreneur requires that you take a broader look at yourself and recognize your strengths and shortcomings. If you've been running your own business for the wrong reasons, you might just have to scrap your entire plan and return to a regular job, even though there will be some people who won't like it.

So if you're having trouble, it's especially important to evaluate what's gone wrong quickly, so you can retool and concentrate on what will make you feel that being an entrepreneur is definitely worth it, or go back to what really works for you.

Marketing

◆

MARKETING IS a term that makes a good number of home-based publishers uncomfortable. Nevertheless, it is one aspect of publishing that they need to know and use intimately in order to survive in the business.

Close your eyes and think: What does marketing mean to you? Most people think of advertising and not much else. You may envision expensive, glossy ad campaigns on TV and in national magazines, and believe there's either something mystical or highly scientific about the ability to draw in customers on the strength of just words and pictures.

You don't need a degree in marketing to sell your products effectively. In fact, you can sell your products better than a professional, because you know your business best. So, if you're thinking of hiring somebody else to do your marketing just to get the job off your hands, forget about it. Just as no one else will handle your guests like you will, so too you're the best person to promote your business. After all the time and money you'll spend on starting your home-based publishing company, you probably regard it as your baby. So who else is better able to convey the attachment and love you have for it to others?

Marketing can actually be fun—you just have to think of it as one of your most creative tasks. In fact, the more creative you are, the more business you'll be able to pull in.

As the owner of a home-based publishing business, you have two big advantages over the big guys: speed and innovation. Many times, a marketing idea at a big corporation has to be approved by hundreds of people before it sees the light of day. By that time, it's usually become so bland as to be ineffective. Needless to say, this big company procedure also takes an inordinate amount of time.

But the way you market your business is different. You're small enough to be able to come up with an idea and to have it in place the same day. You can be outrageous or refined, depending on your mood and what you want to accomplish.

The Purpose of Marketing

YOU MAY have a great product, but unless you let people know that you exist, you won't be able to get even one customer. Last I heard, ESP is not generally recognized as an effective marketing technique. "Oh, they'll find out about me somehow," you reply. But *how* are they going to hear about your publications in the first place? More impor-

tantly, how are you going to convince them to buy your book or newsletter once they *do* find out about you? With *marketing*. And how are you going to locate the kinds of people who will be most interested in your publications? Through *marketing*.

"My brochure knocks 'em dead." But how are you going to get it in the hands of potential customers in the first place? It's great if your brochure and other promotional materials really convey what readers can expect if they purchase one of your publications or other products. However, you must first let them know that you exist before they can send you a check.

The purpose of marketing is to develop and execute a number of different strategies that results in prospective customers learning about one of your publications or your company and then convinces them to give you a try.

Always keep in mind that marketing helps you to attract new customers and keeps them purchasing from you year after year. The best thing about loyal customers is the fact that getting them to buy from you again incurs very little additional marketing costs. They're already familiar with the merits of your publications and the integrity of your company, and you don't have to spend time or money trying to convince them of it.

Defining Your Market

ADMITTEDLY, AMERICANS are largely overwhelmed by media messages today, and some research has shown that most people don't pay attention to the majority of the ads they see. But the messages they *do* notice are the ads that address their specific interests. If an organization they belong to recommends a certain product—your book, software program, or other publication—you can bet they're going to listen and respond.

You won't be able to reach everybody who would benefit from your publications, and even if you could, your message is only one of thousands they see and hear every day. The first step is to target your ideal customer. Even though you should work on attracting customers from this initial group, your target audience may also include potential customers in a larger market than you may have imagined. Keeping records about your customers from the beginning can help you to define your customer even more precisely once you've been running your business for awhile.

Defining who your customer is means that you can then narrow down your choice of the avenues you have available to reach them, as well as the methods you use. Ask yourself the following questions:

✦ Who is most likely to buy your product? Describe two other groups of people who would also benefit from your publications.

✦ What magazines and newspapers do they read? What TV shows and radio programs do they prefer, if any?

✦ Which organizations do you think they belong to?

✦ Does their physical location play a role in whether they'd be more likely to buy from your company? For example, does it matter if they live in a city, the suburbs, or a rural area?

✦ What is their income range?

✦ Why will they decide to buy from your company ?

✦ What do you think would make them decide *not* to buy?

✦ What do you think their goals are for 5, 10, and 20 years down the road? How will your home-based publishing business help them to reach their goals?

Writing Your Marketing Plan

WITHOUT A concrete plan to follow, it's easy to let marketing fall to the bottom of your daily and weekly to-do lists, or even to forget about it entirely. One way to make marketing your business tolerable and even sometimes enjoyable is to map out a specific plan each year. If you say that in March it's time to send out your new brochure to current customers and that your budget that month allows for it, you'll do it.

Like a business plan, a marketing plan is a blueprint for the months ahead, as well as a way to evaluate what has and hasn't worked for you in the past.

When drawing up your marketing plan, make sure you have enough lead time for the special events and promotions you're planning. For instance, it's never too early to think about Christmas if you intend to market your business in national magazines. In fact, the best time to send a press kit to a national magazine about your annual activities is in July. Just be sure to send photos from last year's holiday celebrations.

Developing a marketing plan can be as simple as writing up the goals you'd like to achieve in the next six to twelve months or it can be complicated, containing market and revenue projections as well as the percentage of market share you'd like to take from your competitors.

In your marketing plan you need to define your purpose. You also need a marketing budget that is both reasonable and aggressive, based on your choice of media, and the methods you plan to use to evaluate the results.

Your marketing plan should be spread out among a variety of long-range opportunities and anticipate events that only happen once a year. But the plan is also meant to be tinkered with. For example, suppose a specific advertising issue comes up in September, or you hear about an idea that has worked wonders for another similar business nearby and you want to try it. You may look at your marketing plan for November and December and see you don't have much scheduled, even though your monthly marketing budget allows for $100. You can use the money from those two months to pay for the project.

There are four different aspects to a marketing plan: the amount of time you will spend, on both a daily and weekly basis; the type of marketing you plan to do, from concentrating on magazine publicity to newspaper ads to revamping your brochure and business cards; the amount of money you want to budget for each month and for the total year; and who's going to carry out each task—for some businesses, only one person will be responsible for writing copy, working with a graphic artist, and doing interviews with the press. Even the smallest home-based publishing business owners spread out the responsibilities to ensure they get everything done and to provide a fresh eye. The type of customer you'd like to attract also enters into each of these aspects, broken down by region, profession, sex, income, and interests.

To draw up your annual marketing plan, you'll have to answer a lot of questions. You'll need to be as complete as possible to design the best marketing plan for your business and to incorporate a little bit from each of the following.

Advertising: Ads in radio, newspaper, TV, magazines, Web sites, ezines, and other media.

Direct Mail: Brochures, newsletters, and e-mail sent to prospective, current, and lapsed customers.

Publicity: Letters, press releases and kits, and follow-up sent to the media in hopes of being featured or mentioned in a roundup or service piece.

Other areas: Special events, trade shows, cooperative ventures with the chamber of commerce and other businesses.

In your notebook, write down your answers to the following questions. Again, be as specific as you can.

TIME

+ How much time do you think you will need to spend each week on marketing?

+ Provide a breakdown of how many hours you'll spend each week on publicity, advertising, direct mail, and other areas. Do you feel this is enough time? Do you think you are planning your time effectively?

+ Would you like to spend more or less time? What would you spend it on, or where would you cut back?

+ When do you project your busiest time of the year to be? How far in advance should you begin planning for the marketing projects that you want to do in order to capitalize on this time of year?

MEDIA

+ In which media would you like to focus the majority of your marketing efforts?

+ What type of marketing brings you the most customers?

+ What kind of customer would you like to see more of? How would you reach them?

BUDGET

+ What percentage of total sales does your marketing budget comprise? How could you increase or decrease that amount? What other categories could you take money from?

+ Would you like to invest more money in one or more categories? Which ones? Why?

EXECUTION

+ Name the person or people who will be responsible for marketing. Is there anyone else you feel comfortable assigning additional duties?

+ What additional tasks could you assign to a staff member?

CUSTOMERS

+ In which area of the country do most of your customers live?

+ Are your customers concentrated in one industry?

+ What type of customer would you like to attract more of? How can you target them?

+ Why would they be attracted to your business?

Think about your answers to these questions for a few days. Is there anything missing?

Finding Prospects

YOU PROBABLY have a good idea of the type of person who is likely to become your long-term customer. How do you go about finding them?

There are numerous ways. You should know, however, that prospects are not the same thing as customers. Even though your publishing business is your baby and everyone around you tells you that it's great and that they'd buy in a minute, only a small percentage of people who write or call for information about your company will actually become customers—and it might take awhile for them to decide to do so.

You must view every prospect as a potential customer and treat him or her with the same respect you'd show one of your paid customers, but you shouldn't be disappointed or surprised when he or she doesn't buy. Think of how many offers you're exposed to each day, or about the number of products that you walk by every time you go to the supermarket. Just as you only buy and try a fraction of what's out there, only a fraction of your prospects will buy or try your product. That is why it's vital that you spell out exactly how they'll benefit if they buy one of your publications.

Because there is so much to chose from, we can't know all there is about every product before we make a decision. This means you must find and convert prospects into paying customers by concentrating on those avenues that your group of defined customers travel.

Marketing is not always advertising, as many people wrongly assume. In fact, advertising is one of the least effective and most expensive ways to find your prospects.

Think about your defined customers and then consider the places you can find them; use some of the above suggestions for a jumping-off point. You'll undoubtedly be able to think of many more.

Cloning and Keeping Good Customers

ONCE YOU get a good customer, hold on tight. Your good customer probably knows other people who could also turn out to be good customers. Word of mouth is probably the most effective kind of marketing there is.

There are a variety of ways you can clone good customers. One way is to ask your current customers whether they know other people who would like to receive information about your company and products. You can include a separate form in your mailings asking each customer or potential customer for names, including space where the customer can fill in the names and addresses of friends. Then you can keep track of any orders that you receive through this referral system, offering the first customer a discount, a technique that will also boost your response rate. I know of one home-based publisher who sends a discount coupon for 10 percent off a future workshop sponsored by the company to current customers and encloses an identical

coupon for the customer to give to a friend.

Treating your repeat customers well is another kind of cloning, since they are likely to come back again and again.

The best way to keep your customers coming back is to continue to market to your targeted group of customers and to be consistent in maintaining the quality of your products and your customer service. After all, one reason why customers reorder from you is because they know what to expect.

Finding the Time

FINDING THE time to market your home-based publishing company and your publications is one of the biggest marketing problems that you'll have. I spend 90 percent of my time on marketing and only 10 percent on writing. Even when I'm under deadline, I still try to do some marketing work every day. You should, too. The next time you say you don't have time to market your business, consider these tips:

◆ Because you need to figure out which marketing techniques are bringing in the most customers, it's important to ask each customer or potential customer how he or she heard about your business or about one of your products. Tabulate this information to determine your rate of return on paid advertising and plan where you will spend your marketing budget in the future. Seeing the exact number of dollars that you have pulled in from each of the previous year's advertisements, promotions, and direct mailings will make your media-buying decisions much easier. It also becomes much easier to say *no* to pesky ad reps whose publications don't work for you.

✦ A lot of marketing involves grunt work: stuffing envelopes, making lists, shuffling through ad rate cards. Do this during slow times of the day or night; it's easier to justify when ten other things aren't demanding your attention.

✦ Examine your slow times, whether it's every Monday or the month of March, and perform maintenance tasks on your slow days.

✦ Hire someone to carry out your plan, if you truly can't find enough time, or give the responsibility to a staff member. One home-based publisher hired a PR consultant who was just starting out. She paid the consultant a below-market rate but tied bonuses into any increased business that resulted from the additional publicity. Some home-based publishers say that novices are better than experts; although they don't have the contacts, they also

don't have a lot of preconceived notions about what's right and what's wrong. With marketing, innovation gets attention.

Advertising on a Budget

WITH ADVERTISING you pay for a certain amount of space or time so you can tell your message to a particular audience. Since you're paying to send the message, you can say almost anything you want—time or space and money are the only factors that limit you.

In fact, because you bought the space, you're obviously selling something, and most people turn right off when someone's trying to sell them something.

The primary mistake that many new publishing entrepreneurs make in their marketing is to rely too heavily on advertising. It's not that advertising doesn't work—in some cases it can pull quite well—but it often turns out to be the most expensive way to reach customers, especially when your one-inch display ad is only one of many on a page.

Advertising is a known entity with a tangible product—but it won't necessarily produce the results you desire. Some advertising is easy: You tell the sales rep what you want to say, write a check, go over the proof, and receive a copy of the magazine or a tear sheet. Spending your own time on promotion—whether it's sending out a press kit or renting a booth at a trade show—is harder and doesn't provide you with a tangible result, like an ad in print. What it will do is provide you with increased exposure among your targeted customers; they'll notice you simply because you'll stand out. After all, the majority of businesses take the easy way out, spending the bulk of their annual marketing budget on advertising and perhaps printing another 1,000 copies of their brochure with what's left over.

Take a look at the ads in your local newspapers and magazines. What do they look like? How do they make you feel? Is there one in the entire publication that makes you want to drop what you're doing, pick up the phone, and call? Probably not. Do the same thing the next time you're watching TV or listening to the radio. Pay close attention to the locally-produced ads. Again, do they make you feel excited about whatever it is the advertiser is trying to sell?

The vast majority of advertising in all media is placed to increase consumer awareness, to let people know that a business exists. This type of advertising can build business for your products, but very slowly. By the time you're able to measure the results from your advertising program, you may have gone out of business. It's also difficult to measure. How often do you go into a store and say that you heard their radio commercial? Unless the owner is a friend of yours, probably never.

Because advertising is so expensive, you can't use it just to let people know you're there. Publicity and other more direct marketing tools exist for this reason, and they're also cheap.

The only reason you should spend money to advertise is to back up a special promotion or discount that's available for a limited time, or to offer customers a chance to respond to your ad and receive something for their efforts. A toll-free number, a discount coupon, or a special incentive will help you to measure how many people responded as the result of your ad. Then you can see whether the ad paid for itself, and whether you should try another ad in a later issue of the magazine.

Home-based publishers sometimes feel pressure from a newspaper or magazine editor to advertise in exchange for a promise to cover their business in an editorial section of the publication. This form of coercion is most likely to occur at smaller publications, where the publisher also serves as the editor, and any conflict of interest between advertising and editorial departments is ignored.

If you do decide to advertise, don't settle for the quoted rate. Always ask, "Is that the best you can do?" If the publication is nearing its closing date and there's still ad space left to fill, the sales rep or ad director might sell you the space at a significant discount. In addition, radio and TV stations and publications frequently offer a special rate to first-time advertisers in the hopes that they'll become regular advertisers. They may also offer a discount if you advertise in a special section or sponsor a certain program. Always ask.

Radio and TV advertising don't usually work for home-based publishing entrepreneurs since your primary audience is far too specific for this broad form of marketing to be effective. It's best to focus on print ads in the publications that you know your target audience read. For instance, I advertised a newsletter that told city dwellers how to move to the country in single-state lifestyle magazines whose readers wanted to live in the country—*Vermont Magazine*, *Vermont Life*, *Montana Magazine*, and a small newsletter called *Vermont Property Owners Report* have brought good results for me.

If you're interested in advertising in a particular publication, call the advertising department and ask for a media kit. You'll probably receive a fat folder with a copy of the magazine, a rate card, and lots of material that shows the demographics of the magazine's readers, comparing the numbers to other, similar magazines. Sift through them and take out an ad on a one- or three-time basis in the beginning. If an ad doesn't pull for you after a couple of times, your response rate sure isn't going to improve after the seventh insertion. So give it a shot if you think it might work and pull it before you start to lose a significant amount of money.

Marketing on the Internet

SINCE 1995, use of the Internet as a business marketing tool has gone through the roof; for small business people, there's almost no way to ignore it as a way to gain exposure for your business.

A lot of attention has been paid to the potential of the Internet as a way to make money, but you can't just toss a Web page up and wait for the orders to pour in. Many potential customers will use your site to perform initial research about your company, then call your toll-free number for a catalog, place an order, and send it via snail mail. At this stage of the game, the Internet is still a novelty and a way for people to get information.

Many big businesses pour thousands of dollars into the development of their Web page, then get most of their satisfaction from the fact that they appear to be a technologically hip company. As a small company, you can't afford to be this complacent. The good news is that by combining traditional marketing methods with some high-tech techniques, your Web page can do more than stand as a bits-and-bytes version of your paper marketing materials.

Before you spend the time and money establishing a presence on the World Wide Web, be clear about your intentions. Many businesses have jumped onto the

Internet because everybody else was doing it. So consider your reasons for going online and whether it will be worth it intrinsically to you, at least in the near future.

Beware of companies that sell advertising space on a Web site and inform you that your ad will reach 30 million people in the course of a month. I don't know of any site that generates that much traffic and besides, that audience is usually spending a lot less time at any one site than they would with another form of media. You're better off spending the money developing your own Web site.

Publicity

PUBLICITY MAY be the best kind of marketing you can't buy. That's because aside from the initial costs of preparing a press release and contacting the media about your new publication, publicity is free. When a writer reviews one of your publications in a magazine or newspaper, or a reporter spotlights your company on radio or TV, it is considered to be an endorsement of your business by that particular medium. You didn't pay someone to be mentioned as you do whenever you take out an ad, and so the audience will naturally respond more favorably.

Editors, writers, and reporters at media large and small will rarely review a publication that they don't care for. First off, they don't have the space, and they don't want to waste their own or their audience's time. In most cases, when you see a publication reviewed in a major magazine, it's likely that the editor or author has weeded out less useful publications in order to give it more space.

As with defining your customer, you must also narrow down the media you wish to reach. Many times, your defined customer will select your media for you. For instance, if your defined customer is interested in the subject you cover in your new book or other publication, he or she probably reads other similar publications. So what you need to do is contact those media and convince the editor or writer that their readers will benefit from finding out about you. Of course, if your topic is too close to theirs, the publication may consider you to be a competitor and permanently freeze you out.

First check the masthead for the name of the editor who usually handles the topic your publication covers, or the writer whose byline regularly appears on stories about your topic. Never contact the editor-in-chief of a large or frequent publication, since he or she will be far too busy to respond to you. The managing editor or an associate editor is a far better choice.

For instance, if you publish a cookbook for working mothers and you're looking for customers, you can send a press kit to all of the women's and parenting magazines, as well as to the food magazines and newspaper editors who handle these subjects. You can also rent mailing lists for this group and send a direct mail piece their way. Or maybe you'll want to go to a busy supermarket, stand at the exit, and hand out sample recipes and a brochure to exhausted-looking women with children in tow. Better yet, if you're good at making a presentation and at public speaking, you might work out a deal with the supermarket to hold an in-store demonstration using foods the manager wants to push and those that fit in with your menus and recipes. Then the store can include a blurb about your appearance in its weekly advertisements and you can do your own promotion the week before by appearing on local TV and radio talk shows and arranging to be interviewed by your local daily and weekly newspapers. You'll also want to arrange to have a reporter cover your demonstration.

There are literally thousands of ways to promote your business and products, but I think you get the idea. But before you do any promotion, you'll need a press kit.

Anatomy of a Press Kit

THERE ARE many aspects to marketing that scare people off—for some it may be feeling uncomfortable with self-promotion, for others, the perceived expense—but one of the most intimidating is the notion of putting together a press kit. Common reactions range from "I don't have thousands of dollars to invest in some fancy press kit." to "What goes in it?" In short, this is a press kit:

+ Cover letter
+ Press release
+ Copy of your brochure and other promotional material that you hand out to guests
+ Bio sheet
+ Press clips
+ Glossy black-and-white photo
+ A folder to put them in

Why should you have a press kit? To make it easier for a writer or producer to do a story—or even help them make the decision to do a story about your business in the first place. Writers and radio and TV show producers often need more information than can be found in a brochure. For print stories, they'll need a photo that's easily reproduced, not a picture from your brochure.

A press kit provides this information in a language that media people understand. The press kit should present the facts—the cake, so to speak—so a writer can concentrate on getting the story—the frosting—from an interview.

Here's a brief rundown of the contents of your press kit.

COVER LETTER

Your cover letter should be brief, no more than a page. The first paragraph should consist of one sentence that draws the reader in. I frequently like to word it in the form of a question. In the next paragraph, answer the question and tell how your publication can help the editor's readers improve their lives in some way. Then tell why you're writing to the editor at this particular time, whether it is to alert the media to a special event or to provide them with an introduction and background material on your publication.

Finally, provide a few story suggestions that fall into that particular media's genre and that don't wholly focus on you.

PRESS RELEASE

A press release should cover the five Ws of newswriting: who, what, where, when, and how. Start with an enticing lead, followed by brief paragraphs that are to the point and provide the media with background information.

BIO SHEET

A bio sheet is your resume in prose format. Sometimes an editor or producer will decide to do a story on your com-
pany or publication based on your own personal history, so it helps if you play up something about your life that is unusual or follows current trends. In fact, start off by making this your headline. For instance, if you've always dreamed of helping people to design their own home gardens, and have finally written and published a book on the subject, then say so, and say it early on.

PAST PRESS CLIPS

Frequently, journalists won't cover a story unless somebody else has done it first. But contrary to popular belief, it's not difficult to get press—in many cases, all you have to do is ask for it. If you're new in town, you have a new publication out, or if you've done something new at your company, that's news and you should contact a reporter about it even if you haven't been written up in the past. Try it; you'll see how easy it is. Try the business editor at your local daily or the features editor at your local community weekly paper for a start.

GLOSSY BLACK-AND-WHITE PHOTO

Though a newspaper will frequently send a photographer to take a picture to accompany a story about you and your publication, some of the smaller papers don't have the budget or the time, and they'll usually publish whatever you send them. A 5 × 7 or 8 × 10 glossy black-and-white photograph—usually a head shot or a picture of you working will do. Don't send color prints or slides unless they're specifically requested. You may want to enclose another shot of you, perhaps a full front shot showing you holding a copy of your book or publication, but it's not necessary.

A Folder

Nothing fancy here, just a plain folder with pockets you can stash all of the above in neatly. Some home-based publishers put a label on the front that lists the name of their new publication along with the name of their publishing company, their town, state, and phone number, but the label isn't essential.

On occasion, a reporter or producer will ask for individual pieces from your press kit. This is typical, so don't be offended that he or she won't want to see your entire masterpiece.

A press kit should be a capsule of your business or publication, designed to make a member of the media think enough of you and your business to want to tell readers or listeners about you. This, of course, is the best kind of advertising you could get.

Direct Mail

Most people refer to direct mail as "junk mail," but the truth is that as Americans' lives become increasingly busy and complex, men, women, and children will be more likely to respond to an offer that they receive in the mail, whether it's for a well-earned vacation or a case of dog food.

The secret to effective direct mail selling is to select a mailing list that will "pull," then to tinker with your sales letter, order form, even the color of the envelope you use until you find the combination that brings in the best response. For entrepreneurs who use direct mail to do even a small percentage of their marketing, this form of marketing is akin to a game of golf: They know they can always score higher, so they never stop obsessing over it. In the case of direct mail, however, a little obsession is a good thing.

A direct mail piece needs to be specifically targeted, since most people don't respond to an unsolicited direct mail offer unless the literature answers all of their questions.

There are hundreds of books that will tell you how to write and design an effective direct mail package, but at the very least, here's what you'll need.

+ **Letter:** It can range from one to four pages, or even more. Experts say the longer the letter, the higher your response will be. Remember that your readers must feel comfortable sending money or a credit card number to a company they've never dealt with before.

✦ **Order form:** Make it easy for people to respond. Look at other order forms or the subscription cards you find in many magazines. Then make sure it fits in a reply envelope.

✦ **Reply envelope:** I usually use a #9 envelope with my return address printed on it that customers can easily slip the card into. Some publishers arrange to pay for the postage, but this can become expensive. I've found that people don't object to using their own stamp, but some mail order experts assert that it cuts down on response.

✦ **An envelope to put it all in:** I put my return address in the upper left-hand corner with a teaser of some kind in the lower left. This brief phrase should entice the recipient to open the envelope, which is sometimes a great challenge, especially if you send your package bulk rate.

With these four pieces, you'll have a bare-bones direct mail package. If you can add a sheet that provides even more information about your publications—perhaps on colored paper—your response rate should increase.

Trade Shows

TRADE SHOWS and expos are a great way to get your business before a large number of people who are ready to buy or deciding what to buy in the future. Though exhibiting at a show requires a lot of planning and money, on a per-prospect basis, a trade show is one of the best ways to meet potential clients, as well as touch base with existing customers.

If you're thinking about exhibiting at a trade show, visit as an attendee first to get an idea of the other exhibitors and of what you could do with a booth. Ask the other exhibitors if they come back to the show year after year—a good sign—and check out the booth layout to see where you'd like to have your booth next year. At some trade shows you can get away with a low-tech, homemade look, but this approach may work against you at a trade show where the emphasis is on costly, high-tech displays. Then, before you send in your deposit for a booth at a trade show, call a few of last year's exhibitors with businesses both similar and different from yours and ask how they did there.

Working with Current Customers

YOU'VE PROBABLY heard that you'll get 80 percent of your business from 20 percent of your customers. There is a lot of truth to this statement, though a lot rides on how you treat the your present customers.

Many times, the best marketing technique to use with current customers—and future ones as well—is to smile. People will hesitate to buy from you again if the experience they had during the transaction was unpleasant, even if you offer a product or service that is exclusive to your area or industry.

With this in mind, what follows are several ideas that can enhance your business with your customer list, as well as with future ones, since your customers are quite likely to tell a colleague about your company—word-of-mouth marketing, which is the best kind of all.

◆ Contrary to popular opinion, the customer is not always right. There are some bad customers out there who are nothing but trouble even though you may bend over backward to make them happy; you're better off not wasting your time. Focus instead on pursuing the majority of customers who have had good experiences with you.

◆ Treat all of your customers like family, taking the time to talk with them and giving them an extra something. If you'd do it for your own family, then you should do it for your customers.

◆ Take advantage of the success that you've had with your current roster of customers by collecting all the testimonial letters that you've received,

and assemble them all in a looseleaf notebook.

◆ You can ensure that first-time customers return and refer others to you by giving them something for free after their first purchase. This can be something expected, like helping a customer make some minor adjustments, or unexpected, like sending a box of chocolates or flowers a week after you've made a major sale to a new customer.

You Are Your Own Best Marketing Tool

EVEN IF your product or service is the best or only one around for miles, if you are not responsive to your own customers, you will lose business. All day, no matter where you go or what you're doing, you are a walking billboard for your business, so make the most of it. Realize that your own role as your business's best marketing tool can be fun and fulfilling at the same time.

When you become the best source of information for consumers, they will become your customers. Sims, the discount clothing retailer, uses as its motto, "An educated consumer is our best customer." Take the time to teach consumers about your business whether they call on the phone or walk in off the street.

And always try to refer customers to other area businesses if you are unable to help them. But first take down their name, address, and phone number, and send them a handwritten note expressing your hope that they found satisfaction. Then extend an invitation to do business with you in the future.

Putting It All Together

◆

YOU NOW have the knowledge and the tools necessary to start your own home-based publishing business. Congratulations!

As you know, you'll be taking a class in entrepreneurship every single day that you're running your business. In fact, it may soon seem like you're getting paid not only to be your own boss, but to also learn the kinds of things you wished were taught in high school and college. Now, if you want to investigate something new for your business you can! And without getting permission.

Every home-based publishing entrepreneur will learn more advanced business methods and practice in his or her own time, depending on his or her temperament and specific focus. However, every new business owner will face some of the following issues, too, so take note.

Tracking Your Progress

HOW WILL you know if your business is growing not only at a pace you can handle but at a reasonable pace that will allow you to reach the goals you've set for yourself? Easy. Check in with your business plan at least once or twice a month to see that you're on track with not only the goals and projects you've set for this month, but to also alert you to upcoming tasks.

Remember, you selected each aspect of your business plan as a way to grow your business, so if one project is taking more time than you had planned, it may throw the rest of your growth timeline off kilter. But that's not necessarily a bad thing. Keep in mind that you developed and wrote your business plan before you had a clue about the demands that your business would place on you. It's an occupational hazard of new entrepreneurs that they tend to take on a lot more than they can handle. That's why it's important to compare your sales figures and other benchmarks with the projections in your business plan. If you discover that you're consistently beneath projection but still meeting your expenses, don't be overly hard on yourself; you're obviously doing fine for a new business. As a result, you may want to revamp some of the other plans and projects you have lined up for the rest of the year; optimism and enthusiasm are natural when you first start to put your plans into motion. Now that you have a better idea of what it's like, you should feel open to adjusting your plans.

Another thing to watch for is where the majority of your sales are coming from. When you first planned your business, perhaps you thought you would tailor one service to four distinct groups of people. But now that you've been in business for several months, you find that more than half of your sales are coming from only one group. There could be several reasons for this. Perhaps it's the time of year in that particular industry where people are particularly alert to your field, and so have noticed your ads and brochures more than your other target groups. Or it may be that the people in this group are more closely knit than the others and have spread the word about you among themselves. Or, face it, it could be that this group of customers were your best bet all along. In any case, there are several things you could do. One is to continue marketing equally to all four groups and hope that the other three just need more time to respond. Or you can step up advertising to the other three groups, figuring that perhaps they need more of a nudge. Or, if you're getting as much business as you can handle from the responsive group, you may want to reach more people in that group and postpone your marketing to a totally new group. In any case, as you've learned in Chapter 17, you need to continue marketing in order to keep your business in the consciousness of your current and prospective customers. One group responding above and beyond the others is a good problem to have.

Networking

YOU OFTEN hear that it's not what you know, it's who you know. When it comes to running your own home-based publishing business, both are important, but with all the tasks you have on your plate, you may find that getting together with other business owners—who are running similar or different ventures than you—is something that doesn't take priority in the course of your busy day.

This is a mistake. Joining a variety of business associations when you're first starting out can be absolutely invaluable in terms of the contacts you can make, as well as the advice you can get for free from more experienced entrepreneurs. The importance of networking for entrepreneurs—long considered to be lone wolves when it came to their businesses—first came up in the 1980s. The good news is that all kinds of trade and professional organizations related to your industry as well as general business associations like the chamber of commerce are reporting large increases in membership. That's great for you because it means you'll have access to that many more experts and mentors.

In fact, many industry associations with local chapters have an informal program where members can volunteer to provide a free hour of consultations to any other member. It's a wonderful way to learn from a seasoned professional in your industry.

It's a good idea to join at least two different trade associations when you first start your business: an association specializing in your industry and a more general regional or statewide organization, like the Rotary, business women's group, or the chamber of commerce. If one doesn't exist, then start your own by placing a notice in the local paper and setting a time to meet at a nearby restaurant. It doesn't take much more effort than that, and you may make some valuable contacts who could help you to grow your business faster than you could if you didn't network.

In addition, as briefly described earlier, many associations produce a regular publication for their members, publish specialized information in print and in software form that addresses particular concerns of business owners in the field, and hold occasional meetings and conventions with informative seminars and chances to network with other members. Many hold conventions with trade show areas where you can visit exhibitors who offer new products—usually at special show discounts—that can also help your business to grow.

The majority of associations—both general and industry-connected—also offer members health and life insurance, credit card acceptance privileges, discounted travel expenses, and other business services at a discount.

All of this expertise comes at a price. Annual memberships can be expensive, as well as meetings and new-member initiation fees, but because these expenses are business-related, they're fully tax-deductible. Most entrepreneurs report that the fees are worth it because of the benefits, networking opportunities, and new ideas they receive to help them enhance their own businesses.

In any case, there are as many different solutions to a sticky business problem as there are people who are tackling that particular problem. Be open and direct with the people in your networking community; not only will you be able to hear some surprising and effective ideas that worked for them, but you may be able to give them some advice as well. And that's when you know you're really an entrepreneur: when another business owner looks to you for advice. It will happen, and when it does, it's a great feeling.

Managing Your Time

IF YOU DON'T manage your time, time will manage you. And that can wreak havoc on the life of an entrepreneur. It's inefficient to be yanked around by the urgency of one project or another, instead of you showing your projects exactly who's the boss.

You know the feeling: You spend the entire day running around from one task to another, answering phones and attending to every interruption, and when it's time to turn off the computer, you look

back on your day and see that you weren't able to check anything off on your to-do list for that day.

You should know that of all the aspects of managing your business, managing the way you spend your time and prioritizing which projects and tasks come first is probably the part of running a business that takes the most time to learn.

When you first get your home-based publishing business up and running, especially if you're not used to juggling projects in a number of diverse categories, you'll need to take baby steps. The first step is to write it all down: every project, every task, even the smallest job. Write down how long you expect to have to devote to the task, along with a deadline, whether imposed by you or your customer. Assign a wrapup date to everything that needs to be done; tasks lacking a deadline tend to live in the nether regions of your schedule, always getting pushed aside for something more urgent. If you know you'll get paid more quickly for certain projects, make sure to bump them up a few places on your list.

As each workday begins, make a conscious effort to spend your time on tasks that you've put priorities on, not reacting to the minor crises that come your way and turn your day into an unproductive mess. You may find this difficult: if a number of people come to you to help them solve their problems, it can make you feel competent and important. But if you add up all of these tiny interruptions, you may find that they eat up more than half of your day.

What's the solution? There are several. First, you can delegate more of the decision-making responsibilities to the people who tend to come to you to make it better. This will make them feel capable and they'll be more likely to take on more responsibility within a short time. You can also make it clear that you are not to be interrupted under any circumstances if the door to your office is closed unless it's a dire emergency, the definition of which is up to you. If you feel you're unable to do this, you may want to spend an afternoon or more each week away from home to catch up on your work. A book editor I know escapes to the reading room at a local college library whenever he needs to catch up on correspondence or read manuscripts.

Making a to-do list every day also helps, but what may be more effective is to keep track of projects, appointments, and deadlines on a large wall calendar so that everyone knows when they can expect the crunch times. You may want to color-code the appointments to indicate priorities: Use green magic marker for casual appointments or to mark the days when it's okay for people to interrupt you, blue for major problems, and red for top priority: they can interrupt your work only if your office building is on fire.

Keeping track of your work and appointments on a wall calendar also helps you to plan your weekly and daily to-do lists; four weeks before a big proposal is due, you can work on other projects while you tinker with the outline for the project, but as the weeks pass, you'll know to turn other work over to others or to put it aside altogether.

For your weekly and daily to-do lists, it's totally up to you to decide whether you want to use a regular daybook, a time-management software package, or a portable personal digital assistant that you can take with you and download into your computer back home. Try each to see what works best for you; the handy thing about using a PDA is that you can set an alarm to remind you of important phone calls to make or meetings you need to attend.

Meetings

MANY PEOPLE—employees and entrepreneurs alike—readily believe that the number-one time wasters in the workplace today are meetings. Whether it's a weekly staff meeting, an appointment with a potential client, or a progress report to a current customer, when you count travel, the time spent waiting for everyone to show up, and the announcements and comments that seem to be a requirement of meetings everywhere, meetings aggravate people because they start thinking of the big pile of work back at the office that has to get done immediately, or else the evening—or weekend—is shot.

Of course, there are certain situations where a face-to-face meeting is almost unavoidable, like when you're meeting with a new client or you need to address some problems with your staff. But you can act to reduce the number of inconsequential meetings you attend in several ways. You'll probably find that others will truly appreciate the opportunity to investigate alternatives.

One is to simply beg off because of your workload. Recommend a focused phone conversation instead, and stress that you'll be able to give your undivided attention and be able to take immediate action after you hang up.

If you are running a service-oriented business where your clients are paying you on a per-project or hourly basis, make it clear that if a regularly scheduled—and reasonable—meeting lasts beyond a predetermined amount of time, you will charge for your time. This may also help your clients to be more focused in the use of their time.

If your meeting will proceed as scheduled, make sure it has a definite start and finish time, and lay out the points that need to be addressed in the very beginning. Keep an eye on the clock and push things along when they seem to be straggling.

To date, the best solution involves technology. If you can get your clients and off-site contractors and staff to agree to video conferencing, your meetings can be as effective as ever. Video cams that transmit over the Internet allow for face-to-face meetings even among people located all over the globe. You'll be able to see and hear each other and pick up on the body language and other nuances that phone conversation and e-mail miss. Plus, you won't have to leave your office.

Undoubtedly, other methods and technologies will arise to help you to manage your time better and still accomplish your goals. Choose your weapon wisely and your business—and sanity—will thrive.

Growing Your Business

SINCE YOU'RE first starting out you may think expanding your business would be a great "problem" to have. Once you get there and have to juggle even more tasks and responsibilities when you don't have enough time to accomplish what's already on your plate, you may yearn for the early days of your business when things were hectic, but you still felt you had everything under control.

You may be getting ahead of yourself. You don't want to grow your business until you have your current accounts and responsibilities under control, or you won't be able to provide your current customers with the excellent service they expect. Then they'll go to a competitor, one who isn't spread so thin.

However, it is possible for you to underestimate the need for your business, and you could be swamped from day one. While some entrepreneurs prefer slow, manageable growth as a way to learn the subtleties of running a business and to give them a chance to grow into it, others believe that rapid growth provides them with a real education of what being a business owner is all about. Besides, say quick-growth proponents, sudden growth may push an entrepreneur who was hesitant about forging ahead.

The key to business growth is first planning for it, then managing it and controlling the rate of expansion. Here are a few of the ways in which you can grow your business:

◆ Increase the geographic area in which you market your business

◆ Adapt your current product and/or service to another niche market

◆ Add more products and/or services

◆ Compete on a higher playing field, pursuing business that large companies assume is theirs

Growth can be controlled; it's possible to put the brakes on if you want to grow your business at a more reasonable pace. One of the ways you can do this is by limiting the number of customers you work with, either by booking them ahead or by telling overflow clients you can't handle them now. You can pass the lead along to one of your networking buddies for brownie points from both sides. You can also limit growth by the prices you charge; by setting higher fees than your competition, you are excluding a certain segment of your market. In some cases, however, you may actually attract *more* customers with higher prices, since to many people higher price is a sign of better quality, and depending on the type of business you're in, exclusivity can be a strong selling point.

A big issue you'll face in growing your home-based publishing business is whether to hire employees or, if you already have help on board, whether you should hire more or contract out additional work if possible. If you're used to doing everything yourself, letting go some of the responsibility—both the big projects and the day-to-day stuff—can be excruciating. Remember about a business being a baby to raise and nurture? In time, under a crushing workload, most entrepreneurs change out of necessity. As you begin to learn about your colleagues, you'll be able to delegate more responsibility to them, leaving more of the stuff that you want to do to you.

Another great "problem" that can actually turn into a big pain is what to do with the extra money generated by business growth. No matter how large their business becomes, some entrepreneurs continue to plow every extra penny back into their enterprise. Others reward themselves with a trophy like a car or a new house, but then return to their old frugal ways.

Of course, you should expect that the Internal Revenue Service will want their share, which is why many entrepreneurs plow the money back into the business; if it's a bona fide business expense, it's a tax deduction, whether you spend the money on an addition to the building, more advertising, or a new employee. At the very least, you should put some of the money aside for those months when times aren't as flush—and they are inevitable.

What's Next?

WHEN AN entrepreneur has established a successful business with happy customers and contented employees he or she often starts thinking about the next venture. If there's one personality trait all entrepreneurs have in common, it's the desire to start new businesses. The challenge of starting a company from scratch is one of the greatest satisfactions in life; you'll see, when you have been in business for awhile, even if you've experienced great ups and downs. These people are known as entrepreneurial entrepreneurs: They're not completely happy

unless they're actively working to start a new business.

Starting and running a business can be addictive. It's very easy to get so caught up in running your home-based publishing business that you have absolutely no desire to spend your waking hours doing anything else. This is precisely why so many business owners spend 80, even 100 hours a week building their businesses, and why some don't hire employees even if they desperately need the help. This is also why so many entrepreneurs end up burned out and discontent with their businesses at some point down the road.

The *what's next?* question can come up even if you're burned out. Running a successful business—or an unsuccessful one, for that matter—is a lot more difficult than it appears. Both new and veteran home-based publishing entrepreneurs frequently underestimate the amount of work the business will require while overestimating the money that the business will generate. An entrepreneur who's caught between these two aspects is headed for a head-on crash.

On the whole, entrepreneurial entrepreneurs typically spend five years on one business before moving on to something else. You'll know it's time to look at your next step when:

◆ You no longer become excited about a new development in your industry

✦ You work through the holidays

✦ You've lost your enthusiasm for work and play

✦ You can't remember the last time you woke up feeling refreshed

Many home-based publishing business owners who love what they're doing may feel one or all of these symptoms at one time or another, but you need to move when your current venture no longer presents a challenge. Pay attention to the signs, take care of yourself and your business, and try to spend at least some time each week thinking about something besides work.

Sample Business Plan

◆

Litterature
Williams Hill Publishing
Grafton, New Hampshire 03240
A Business Plan by Lisa Shaw

Statement of Purpose

L ITTERATURE IS a company that produces greeting cards for cats and dogs and for the people in their lives. It is operated as a division of Williams Hill Publishing in Grafton, New Hampshire, a company that has published newsletters, and produced software, and that currently publishes books about New England and conducts publicity campaigns for other small businesses. This business plan will serve as a blueprint to steer the company after the first quarter of business, and as projections for the first two full years of business.

Section One: The Business

DESCRIPTION OF THE BUSINESS

Litterature is a company that produces greeting cards designed to be sent from people to pets, pets to people, and pets to pets. Fully three-quarters of the cards currently available can also be used by people to send to other people. Litterature was launched with 101 different cards in quantities of 500 each, available through a 28-page catalog that served both wholesale markets and direct sales to consumers. Each card retails for $2.00 and wholesales for $1.00. To serve the wholesale markets, display cards to place in each pocket of a greeting card rack—such as Dog Birthday or Cat Sympathy—were also created, in addition to a topper with the company name to place atop each rack. A graphic designer was hired to scan each card, clean it up for the printer, and then send it to film, in addition to laying out and designing the catalog, rack cards, and toppers. This layout was then transferred to a Web page with a URL of www.litterature.com.

In addition to the greeting cards, Litterature produces and sells other pet-related objects, including books, party kits, personalized Christmas stockings, mugs, T-shirts, writing kits (a rubber-stamp paw print and ink pad), and other products that enhance and supplement the greeting cards in the wholesale and retail markets. Future products include more varieties of cards, wrapping paper, gift enclosures, gift baskets, customized cards and rolls of perforated postcards for pet professionals, fund-raising jewelry for humane societies, and a line of books about cats and dogs.

Litterature utilizes antique postcards as the basis of the art for the cards in order to keep production costs down. The postcards are in the public domain, copyright-free, and cost much less to produce than hiring an artist to create original art. The categories include adoption, birth announcements, happy birthday, happy holidays, good cat/dog, congratulations, missing you, humorous, sorry, get well soon, sympathy (so far, our biggest seller), blank cards, thank-you cards to send to pet professionals, and practice-building cards that vets, groomers, and pet sitters can send to their clients.

A strong selling point of the cards is that they are produced on recycled paper and that 10 percent of the revenues generated by Litterature are donated to humane societies and other animal welfare associations.

DESCRIPTION OF THE MARKET

Studies report that there are approximately 70 million dogs and 70 million cats kept as pets in the United States today. In talking with cat and dog owners on the Internet and in person, I've discovered that many of them already send greeting cards to their pets, except that they have to alter cards for people so that they more accurately represent the purpose of the card. Indeed, a study conducted by the American Animal Hospital

Association in 1996 found that 62 percent of pet owners sign a letter or card to be sent to another person or pet, 50 percent of pet owners celebrate their pet's birthday, and 79 percent of pet owners give their pet a present for their birthday and for the holidays.

Litterature currently pursues customers in the following areas:

✦ Publicity in pet-oriented publications as well as mainstream media

✦ Appearances at trade shows, pet shows, and crafts fairs with booth rentals

✦ Co-op marketing with other pet-related small businesses, such as, providing a catalog for the manufacturer of Video Catnip or the manufacturer of Vermont Animal Cookies to enclose when they fulfill an order

✦ Direct marketing to selected rented lists, both trade and consumer

✦ Marketing with a Web page and links to other dog and cat Web pages

✦ Wholesaling to gift shops, pet shops, bookstores, and catalog companies that sell pet products through our present network of 50 reps in New England, the Midwest, the Pacific Northwest, California and the Southwest, and North and South Carolina

✦ Bulk single-card sales to vets, kennels, and other animal care professionals

DESCRIPTION OF THE COMPETITION

There are literally thousands of greeting cards with cats on them, but most are designed to be given to humans, not cats. The handful of companies producing greeting cards for cats or dogs fall into one of two categories: They are either small part-time crafts businesses with a line of 10 to 20 cards or a line extension of a corporation like Hallmark or American Greetings. In the *Boston Globe* on December 9, 1996, Diane White devoted her column to the topic of greeting cards for pets: "Have Fido and Fluffy Sent Out All Their Greeting Cards?" (Carlton Cards produces 50 cards, while Hallmark publishes 97 cards. We beat both of them by producing 101 different cards with our first line.) This was the second time in one month that Litterature was written up in the *Globe*; the first article, "Next Time Rover Scares a Postman, Just Hide His Mail," appeared in the Sunday, November 3, 1996, New Hampshire Weekly edition of the *Globe*.

DESCRIPTION OF THE MANAGEMENT

Lisa Shaw has served as publisher and editor at Williams Hill Publishing, which has produced two successful newsletters—*Sticks and Travel Marketing Bulletin*—

and a computer software program entitled *The Business Traveler's Guide to Inns & B&Bs*. She has also written 25 books for other publishers, including *The Quotable Cat*, published in 1992 by Contemporary Books, and *The Cat on My Shoulder*, a book about famous writers and their cats, published in hardcover by Longmeadow Press in 1992 and brought out in paperback by Avon in 1993.

She has conducted marketing and publicity campaigns for other publishers, and her efforts for Williams Hill Publishing have resulted in editorial mentions in the *Wall Street Journal*, *USA Today*, *New York Magazine*, *Self Magazine*, *Playboy*, the Associated Press national newswire, and many other national publications.

She will continue to write books for other publishers and to conduct publicity campaigns for other small businesses to generate revenue to help to build Litterature.

DESCRIPTION OF THE PERSONNEL

Williams Hill Publishing will continue its tradition of farming out extra work to independent contractors and small businesses that specialize in the services that Litterature will require. An 800-number order-taking service is already in place, orders are packed in-house, and a local printer produces the cards, envelopes, catalogs, rack cards, and toppers.

For the first year, I expect not to hire any employees. I should be able to handle rep management as well as continuing to fulfill orders in-house. Should this start to consume too much time, I will contract an outside fulfillment company to pack and ship wholesale and retail orders.

MARKETING EFFORTS

The early marketing efforts at Litterature have been extensive. They include the following:

✦ Media publicity to encourage direct sales to consumers, help reps present the line with credibility, and increase visibility to retailers and other wholesale markets. Press clippings are attached and include the *Wall Street Journal*, several major-market drive-time radio station interviews (Chicago; St. Louis, which brought over 200 inquiries from a five-minute interview; Toledo), hundreds of appearances in newspapers all across the country (complete with 800 number and ordering information) from the *San Francisco Chronicle* to the *Nashville Tennessean* to the *Chicago Tribune*. Magazines that have mentioned the cards include *Family Circle*, *TWA Ambassador*, *Publishers Weekly*, and *Cats Magazine*. TV shows that have mentioned the cards include *The Tonight Show*, *The Fox*

News Channel, and TNN's *Prime Time Country*.

✦ Specialized mailings to 200 sales reps and rep groups in the gift and pet markets resulted in the signing of 50 different reps all across the country, including the West, which I believe is the area of the country that will become the largest customer base for Litterature and its products.

✦ Trade show exhibits at two major pet industry shows in the fall (H. H. Backer Christmas Show in Chicago in October 1996; World Wide Pet Supply Association Northern California trade show in San Francisco in November 1996) exposed the Litterature line to pet shop owners, veterinarians, groomers, and the pet industry media. The article about Litterature that appeared in the February issue of *Cats Magazine* was a direct result of meeting the magazine's editor at the Backer show.

✦ Direct mailings to catalogs that feature cat and dog merchandise. Nothing solid yet, but many of our reps sell to catalogs, so the repetition factor should help here.

✦ Direct mailings to the owners of pet cemeteries.

✦ Direct mailings to other pet manufacturers for co-op marketing projects and bulk premium sales.

✦ Direct mailings to veterinarians in New Hampshire, Vermont, and Maine increased exposure of the cards. Our regional sales reps visit veterinarians on their rounds and are regularly met with name recognition.

✦ Links to our Web site from other pet-related Web pages. So far, Internet orders are slowly trickling in, about one a week, but having a Web site definitely caters to those who don't want to wait a few days to receive a print catalog in the mail.

✦ Advertisements in trade publications, such as *Publishers Weekly*. Bookstores are turning out to be a great market for the cards, with the Dartmouth Bookstore in Hanover, New Hampshire, and The Tattered Cover in Denver, Colorado, making wholesale purchases in December 1996.

Marketing efforts in all areas will continue to grow throughout the first two years and beyond. Future marketing plans include focusing on specific groups: dog and cat clubs, shelter fund-raising programs, trade show exhibits at veterinary and grooming conferences, and primarily increasing the wholesale avenues for Litterature.

SUMMARY

Williams Hill Publishing expects that Litterature will be a thriving business within two years, with 100 sales reps and distributors increasing the reach of the greeting cards into the retail market. Once direct sales have been established, Litterature will spend time focusing on bulk markets like vets and kennels, which will become the financial backbone of the company.

In 1997, Litterature will also begin producing its own line of cat and dog books, to be distributed directly to its customer list and through wholesale reps to bookstores, pet shops, and gift markets. Litterature's umbrella company, Williams Hill Publishing, will also introduce its first line of books on New England topics in March 1997, beginning with *New Hampshire vs. Vermont*, to be followed by *Free New England*, a guide to free and inexpensive events and attractions throughout the region, scheduled for publication in the spring of 1998. The first two titles from Litterature are planned: *Innside the Animal House: A Guide to Cats & Dogs at New England's Inns & B&Bs* and a guide to starting and running a pet-oriented business.

The company also has a regional pet magazine on the drawing board, entitled *New England Pet*, a monthly tabloid that would be solely supported by advertising and distributed free in pet shops, veterinarian offices and groomer shops, bookstores, and other pet-related venues throughout New England. This publication would help to promote Litterature products and forge strong relationships with other businesses in the pet industry.

Section Two: Financial Data

EXPECTED USE OF INITIAL INVESTMENT

Williams Hill Publishing has invested $33,925 from March 1996 through January 1997.

$12,500	Printing of 101 card designs, 500 of each card and envelope
$6,000	Printing of 15,000 catalogs
$4,085	Printing of rack display and topper cards
$5,000	Booth rental and travel expenses to display at two trade shows
$1,000	Postage
$1,500	Phone expenses
$840	Copier rental for six months
$3,000	Miscellaneous expenses
$33,925	Total

Williams Hill Publishing expects that once the network of sales reps becomes fully operational in February 1997, it will take three to four months before regular revenue from wholesale accounts is being generated. We plan to add reps until the entire country is covered; we've acquired 50 reps in 25 states in just two months. The minimum wholesale order is $150, with 20 percent paid to the reps as a wholesale commission; wholesale accounts pay for all shipping expenses.

Projected revenue is as follows.

If each of 45 reps sells two Litterature orders each month, the monthly gross revenue will be $13,500 (45 x 2 x $150). The rep commission paid out will be $2,700, which leaves $10,800. These revenues should be generated by April or May. Since I plan to double the number of Litterature reps across the country by the end of 1997, for a total of 90 reps, the revenues cited here will double: monthly gross will be $27,000 (90 x 2 x $150 each), with rep commissions totaling $5,400.

Projected sales from consumer markets as well as specialty markets such as, premium sales, bulk and rack sales to vets will contribute to the revenue stream, but compared to wholesale revenue will represent 10 to 15 percent of gross revenue; this market primarily serves to increase exposure of Litterature to the general public. In addition, I hope to be able to phase out direct sales to consumers within 12 to 18 months, after the rep network is able to saturate the retail market with greeting cards and our other products.

Williams Hill Publishing expects first-year revenues of $45,000, with most of that figure generated through wholesale markets. This includes sales of our books and other ancillary products, like Christmas stockings, birthday party kits, and feline and canine writing kits, as well as direct sales to consumers and bulk sales to pet professionals.

Sample Marketing Plan

✦

Marketing Plan for Litterature

WILLIAMS HILL Publishing expects that approximately 20 percent of the annual revenues generated by Litterature will be spent on marketing in the first year. We project first-year revenues at $45,000, with most of that figure generated through direct sales. Sales of books and other ancillary products such as Christmas stocking packages for cats will add another $5,000 to the total.

Litterature will really expand in 1997, riding on a wave of positive publicity and inquiries from sales reps and distributors so that wholesale revenues will begin to take hold, as well as bulk sales to vets and kennels.

The four major methods of marketing are detailed in the business plan. What follows is a month-by-month marketing plan.

First Month

Mail press kit, catalogs, and sample cards to 400 media names. One week later, make follow-up calls. Approximate cost, including printing, postage, phone calls, and labor: $600. Send catalog and sample cards to self-generated in-house mailing list, open a Litterature Web page, and provide links to and make announcements on other cat-related Internet sites. Approximate cost: $300.

Second Month

Visit local shops to sell selected cards. Provide them with racks and set up accounts. Approximate cost: $200.

Third Month

Book a booth at two major cat shows, one in New England and one in the New York metropolitan area. Booth rentals: $500. Travel expenses: $500. Total: $1,000.

Fourth Month

Rent a partial (5,000 name) list of veterinarians. Prepare a simple letter inviting them to set up an account, paid by check or credit card to simplify bookkeeping and provide immediate cash, and to purchase single-topic greeting cards they can send to their clients. Check results before mailing to larger list. Mailing list rental: $250 ($50 per 1,000 names). Printing: $1,400. Postage: $1,000 (bulk rate at local mailing house). Handling: $200 ($40 per 1,000 pieces). Total: $2,850.

Fifth Month

Rent a partial (5,000 name) list of kennels and groomers. Prepare a simple letter inviting them to set up an account, paid by check or credit card to simplify bookkeeping and provide immediate cash, and to purchase single-topic greeting cards

they can send to their clients. Check results before mailing to larger list. Mailing list rental: $250 ($50 per 1,000 names). Printing: $1,400. Postage: $1,000 (bulk rate at local mailing house). Handling: $200 ($40 per 1,000 pieces). Total: $2,850.

Sixth Month

Take time to tabulate figures to see which marketing effort performed best.

Seventh Month

Do another press mailing to the original media list of 400 names plus 100 new names to be targeted. Include press clippings from media who have already mentioned Litterature and alert them to upcoming press appearances. Approximate cost: $750.

Eighth and Ninth Month

Make follow-up calls for the press mailing. Approximate cost: $100.

Tenth Month

Book a booth at two major cat shows, one in New England and one in the New York metropolitan area. Frame press clippings and display them at booth. Booth rentals: $500. Travel expenses: $500. Total: $1,000.

Eleventh Month

Arrange with as many catalogs and mail-order retailers as possible to enclose a Litterature catalog whenever they fill an order. Provide them with catalogs and pay them 25 cents for each catalog they send. Approximate cost: $300.

Twelfth Month

Take stock of which marketing effort worked best in the last year. Call best cus-tomers and ask for feedback about future projects. Draw up marketing plan for next year. Approximate cost: $100 (for phone calls). Total annual marketing expenses: $10,500.

Resources

✦

Booklets

"How to Write and Market Booklets for Ca$h," Paulette Ensign. Eighty-page blueprint of how she sold over 400,000 copies in two languages of a 16-page tips booklet, all without spending a penny on advertising. $35.00, shipping included.

"110 Ideas for Organizing Your Business Life," Paulette Ensign. Sixteen-page tips booklet that includes information on paper, time, and space management. $5.00, shipping included.

Tips Products International, Organizing Solutions, Inc.
12675 Camino Mira Del Mar, #179
San Diego, CA 92130
http://www.realvoices.com/booklets
E-mail: booklets@realvoices.com
Phone: (619) 481-0890
Fax: (619) 793-0880

Books

The Complete Publisher's Resource Manual
Linda Able
Florida Academic Press, $22.95
POB 540
Gainesville FL 32602
(352) 332-5104

The Prepublishing Handbook
Patricia J. Bell
Cat's-paw Press, $12.00
9561 Woodridge Circle
Eden Prairie, MN 55347

How to Become a Bestselling Author
Stanley J. Corwin
Writer's Digest Books, $14.95

The Huenefeld Guide to Book Publishing
John Huenefeld
Mills & Sanderson Publishers, $29.95

1001 Ways to Market Your Books
John Kremer
Ad-Lib Publications, $19.95
51 North Fifth Street
Fairfield, IA 52556

The Self-Publishing Manual
Dan Poynter
Para Publishing, $19.95
P.O. Box 2206
Santa Barbara, CA 93118-2206

The Complete Guide to Self-Publishing
Tom and Marilyn Ross
Writer's Digest Books, $18.95

1001 Ways to Market Yourself and Your Small Business
Lisa Shaw
Perigee Books, $12.95

Kitchen Table Publisher: How to Publish City Magazines, Regional Magazines, Tourism Guides, Newcomer Guides, Chamber of Commerce "Quality of Life" Magazines, Weekly Newspapers, Free Circulation Shoppers
Tom Williams, Ph.D.
Venture Press
(954) 796-0104

Poet Power! The Practical Poet's Complete Guide to Getting Published (and Self-Published)
Tom Williams, Ph.D.
Venture Press
(954) 796-0104

Newsletters

Book Marketing Update
Bradley Communications
POB 1206
Lansdowne PA 19050-8206
(800) 989-1400, ext. 432

Book Marketing & Publicity
5900 Hollis Street
Ste R2
Emeryville, CA 94608-2008
(800) 959-1059

Organizations

Publishers Marketing Association
2401 Pacific Coast Highway, Suite 102
Hermosa Beach, CA 90254
(310) 372-2732

SPAN
Communication Creativity
POB 909
Buena Vista CO 81211
(800) 331-8355

Web Sites

Kitchen Table Publisher
www.PubMart.com

Aeonix Publishing Group, Publishing
Production and Consulting, Cover and
Book Design, Layout, and Production
www.aeonix.com

BookIdea Magazine
www.bookidea.com

Software

PUB123
Back-office software system for small
publishers
www.adams-blake.com; abpub@ns.net

Index

✦

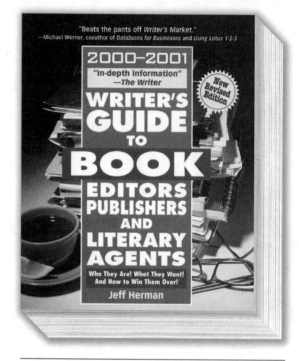

Crime Does Pay!

True crime and suspense stories make a killing at the box office, on the bestseller lists, and on TV. Both new and experienced writers have found that they can master the special skills required to make crime pay—in book and movie contracts. This book shows you how you, too, can:

- **Find and develop compelling true crime stories from everyday sources**

- **Dig out the facts and put them on paper**

- **Fashion your story for books, TV, or movies**

- **Market your story for maximum profit**

- **And much, much more!**

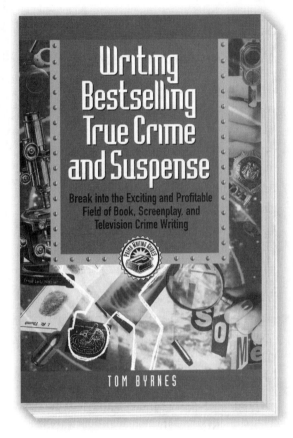

ISBN 0-7615-1026-5 / Paperback
336 pages / U.S. $17.00 / Can. $22.95

PRIMA

To order, call (800) 632-8676 or visit us online at www.primalifestyles.com

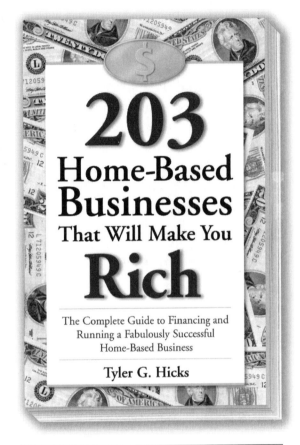

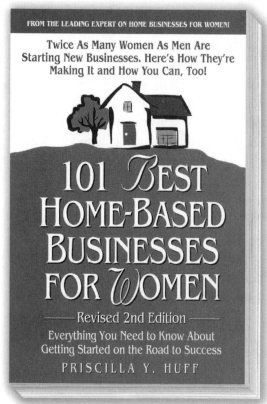

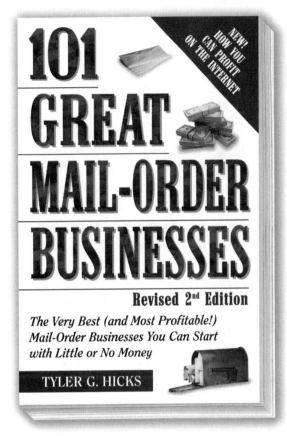

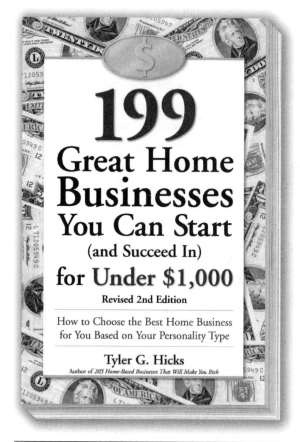

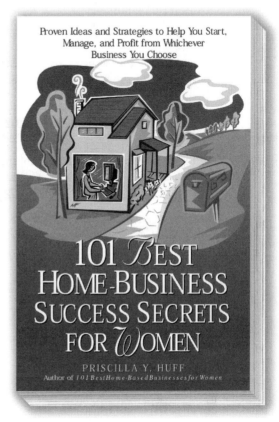

To Order Books

Please send me the following items:

Quantity	Title	U.S. Price	Total
_____	101 Best Home-Based Businesses for Women, Revised 2nd Edition	$ _____	$ _____
_____	101 Best Home-Business Success Secrets for Women	$ _____	$ _____
_____	101 Great Mail-Order Businesses, Revised 2nd Edition	$ _____	$ _____
_____	199 Great Home Businesses You Can Start (and Succeed In) for Under $1,000, Revised 2nd Edition	$ _____	$ _____
_____	203 Home-Based Businesses That Will Make You Rich	$ _____	$ _____
_____	I Love the Internet, but I Want My Privacy, Too!	$ _____	$ _____
_____	Writer's Guide to Book Editors, Publishers, and Literary Agents, 2000–2001	$ _____	$ _____
_____	Writer's Guide to Book Editors, Publishers, and Literary Agents, 2000–2001 (CD-ROM)	$ _____	$ _____
_____	Writing Bestselling True Crime and Suspense	$ _____	$ _____

Subtotal	$ _____
7.25% Sales Tax (CA only)	$ _____
7% Sales Tax (PA only)	$ _____
5% Sales Tax (IN only)	$ _____
7% G.S.T. Tax (Canada only)	$ _____
Priority Shipping	$ _____
Total Order	$ _____

FREE
Ground Freight in U.S. and Canada

Foreign and all Priority Request orders:
Call Customer Service
for price quote at 916-787-7000

By Telephone: With American Express, MC, or Visa,
call 800-632-8676, Monday–Friday, 8:30–4:30
www.primapublishing.com

By E-mail: sales@primapub.com

By Mail: Just fill out the information below and send with your remittance to:
Prima Publishing ▪ P.O. Box 1260BK ▪ Rocklin, CA 95677

Name _____

Address _____

City _____ State _____ ZIP _____

MC/Visa/American Express# _____ Exp. _____

Check/money order enclosed for $ _____ Payable to Prima Publishing

Daytime telephone _____

Signature _____